Fundamentals *of* **Marketing**
for the Real Estate Professional

Doris Barrell • Mark Nash

Dearborn™
Real Estate Education

This publication is designed to provide accurate and authoritative information in regard to the subject matter covered. It is sold with the understanding that the publisher is not engaged in rendering legal, accounting, or other professional service. If legal advice or other expert assistance is required, the services of a competent professional person should be sought.

President: Roy Lipner
Publisher: Evan M. Butterfield
Associate Publisher: Louise Benzer
Development Editor: Tony Peregrin
Managing Editor, Production: Daniel Frey
Quality Assurance Editor: David Shaw
Creative Director: Lucy Jenkins

Contents

7 Putting It All in Practice: Field Exercises 163

Making the Most of Your First Line of Marketing—You!

As the Cheshire Cat once told Alice, "If you don't know where you're going any road will take you there." The same applies in marketing. If you don't know what your destination is, it doesn't make much difference what route you take. If you do know your goals and where you want to go, you will need a road map in order to get there.

In marketing, that road map is a well-thought-out, detailed plan. You must first set your goals, then determine what actions must be taken in order to reach those goals. The actions become your marketing plan execution. The journey begins, and at the end you may find that you have made a few wrong turns along the way, but you will eventually arrive exactly where you hoped you would.

Look backward to see which paths brought you closest to your destination. Look forward to seek new directions and opportunities. Then when you know precisely where you want to go, you will also know exactly the roads to take to get there!

YOUR GREATEST ASSET—YOU!

In upcoming chapters we will talk about all of the tools and techniques that successful real estate agents have been using for years. We'll also spend time looking at the latest in 21st-century technology. But in the long run, all of these are only tools. Agents enjoy success in real estate marketing by using the tools. Never discount the importance of your role. It is your knowledge, your energy, your enthusiasm, and your dollars that go into making your real estate marketing plan a winner.

Included in the 2002 National Association of REALTORS® (NAR) *Profile of Home Buyers and Sellers* is a survey revealing where homebuyers obtained information about properties they were interested in purchasing (see Table 1.1). In the majority of cases, no matter which of the various media was referenced (newspaper ad, the Internet, the Yellow Pages), the real estate agent was the most important source of information. See how valuable you are!

YOUR PERSON-TO-PERSON SPHERE OF INFLUENCE

One of the most effective marketing tools—and the one that is most often ignored—is your own sphere of influence. Sam Young, probably best known for his book *Strategies for Success in Real Estate* (Reston Publishing Company, 1983) frequently taught a class on how to set up a "Sphere of Influence" and make it work. Sam always began by challenging everyone in the class to make a list of over 200 people that they know on a first-name basis. This list becomes the core of a sphere of influence database. Keeping in touch with people whom you already know is easier, more

TABLE 1.1 / Sources Used by Homebuyers in Home Search, 2001

Real Estate Agent	79%	Builders	11%
Newspaper Ad	41%	Television	4%
Internet	41%	Knew the Seller	5%
Yard Sign	32%	Relocation Company	2%
Homes Book/Magazine	24%	Yellow Pages	1%
Friend/Neighbor/Relative	21%	Other	1%

pleasant, and generally more effective than any type of cold-calling or general mailing. Remember that the point is not necessarily to see if the names on your original list want to buy, sell, or lease real estate. The purpose for keeping in touch with these people is to promote yourself and your particular area of expertise so that they will think of you when someone in their circle of friends and family has real estate needs.

Making Your Sphere-of-Influence List

Your list of 200 people can be broken down into three groups:

1. **The A Group** are those who will actively promote business for you. (Usually limited to your mother and your best friend!)
2. **The B Group** are those who will bring up your name whenever they hear someone mention that they are thinking about buying, selling, or leasing property.
3. **The C Group** are those who will give your name if someone asks them directly for a recommendation for a real estate agent.

The goal is to move as many people as you can from the C Group up into the B Group. There will never be many people in the A Group, but a strong B Group automatically thinking of you whenever they hear the words "real estate" will provide you with a steady stream of business for many years.

Enlarging the Sphere

Just one referral a year from each of their original 200 people would make any agent smile! But consider the potential here: each of your 200 contacts also has at least 200 contacts. What if even just 1 out of the 200 names on their list was referred to you? Your sphere of influence would expand by a quantum leap.

As your real estate business develops, all satisfied clients and customers should automatically be added to your sphere of influence list. Whenever you send out a just listed/sold card, a newsletter, an invitation to an open house or homebuyer seminar, or any other type of mailing, be sure to send one to everyone on your list. This helps keep your name in their minds whenever one of their acquaintances mentions that they are interested in buying or selling real estate. And, of course, be sure to make contact with each of your past customers and clients on the anniversary of their closing.

Making the Contact. It does not matter whether you make these contacts with a telephone call, e-mail, handwritten note, or one of the prepared note cards now available. The point is to make regular contact, preferably four times per year. Remembering that person's birthday or anniversary is always a winner. Seasonal holidays provide a great reason, but you might make your message stand out by getting in touch on the less celebrated days like St. Patrick's Day, Columbus Day, or Chinese New Year. There are many computer software programs available to help you maintain your contact information and serve as a reminder when it is time to make that call or send an e-mail or written note.

Contacting Your Sphere

A great excuse for contacting those on your sphere of influence list is to ask for their opinion on the current real estate market. Ask if they think consumer confidence is going up or down and why. A random survey of 200 people does not provide indisputable statistics, but it is adequate enough to see an overall picture. Other survey topics could include questions such as the following:

- Which room in the house is the most important to you?
- How many bedrooms and bathrooms would you prefer?
- Would you rather live in a more urban, suburban, or rural area?
- On your next move, would you prefer a larger or smaller house?

You could also ask if they have seen the National Association of REALTORS® ads on TV. Do they think these ads have had any impact on the general public's attitude toward the value of using a professional real estate agent?

Conducting a survey of opinions from those on your sphere-of-influence list is very different from a survey taken from the general public. These people know you through a personal or business relationship. They will not need to be bribed with incentives or promised a reward for responding. A survey is just an easy way for you to find a reason for making contact. If you are making the contact in person or over the telephone, you will have instant response. If you choose to send out your questionnaire by mail, you will want to keep it very easy to answer and enclose a self-addressed, stamped envelope for its return.

Using Survey Results in Marketing

The data accumulated from your survey can be used in preparing a marketing plan for your new listings. If the survey shows that 9 out of 10 people think that two or more bathrooms are important, write ad copy stressing the fact that this older Colonial home does actually have two full baths on the bedroom level plus a powder room on the first floor and a roughed-in bath in the basement. If the survey indicates that a majority of people today are interested in updated kitchens and energy-saving features in a home, your advertising dollars will be better spent stressing the brand-new appliances and storm windows than the fact that the house has a large yard with apple trees and three brick fireplaces in the house.

Evaluating survey results about the general public's image of real estate agents also could be the basis for a marketing plan for promoting your services. Can you promise the client a high standard of ethical practice? Are you willing to assure individual attention and full representation in your role as buyer agent? Will you be able to provide information on a variety of mortgage loan products in order to find the one most beneficial for the purchasers?

Networking Groups

A slightly different spin on the sphere of influence is the networking group. The members of your sphere are those you already know through some other relationship. The networking group is made up of those you seek out in order to profit by personal promotion within the group. A networking group is generally made up of a small group of professionals who meet on a regular basis to exchange ideas and to support one another in business.

One group may be totally diversified in different fields; i.e., a doctor, a lawyer, a CPA, a dentist, a stockbroker, etc. Another group could be more real estate oriented; i.e., a loan officer, title agent, real estate attorney, builder, home inspector, handyman, etc. A third type of networking group is one made up of all real estate professionals. Some agents might think this is not a good idea because of competition issues, but a well-selected group of agents and brokers who represent different areas of the real estate business or different geographic areas within a large metropolitan area can provide an excellent source for promoting both yourself and your properties.

CREATING AN IMAGE

The first component of marketing is creating an image. If you want to establish a clear image in the minds of your sphere of influence, networking groups, and real estate consumers, you must first be able to see that image in your own mind. Do you see yourself as an accredited buyer's agent who is great at working with first-time homebuyers? Are you proficient in another language and believe you have much to offer to persons in that language group? Do you believe that you are particularly empathetic to the needs of senior citizens? Have you become an expert in the field of mortgage lending? Regardless of the special area of expertise or ability that you envision as part of your image, you always want to project the image of a successful real estate professional; knowledgeable, caring, honest, and ethical in business practice.

Getting Really Personal!

When projecting the image of a successful real estate agent, remember that you never get a second chance at a first impression. Keep that in mind when you select your clothing for the day, the condition of your automobile, or the way you talk.

All too often the image portrayed in the movies and on TV of the real estate agent is very unflattering. The real estate woman wears five-inch heels, a short-skirted, tight-fitting suit, loads of gold jewelry, and has a highly teased hairdo. She may sound totally inane, gushing ridiculously about the property she is marketing. The real estate man is often portrayed as a fast-talking, super-pushy guy, driving a big Caddy, who is obviously only interested in making a buck at the expense of the consumer. Presumably you want to portray the image of a highly skilled professional who follows a high standard of practice and conducts business in an ethical way at all times. Can this image be portrayed when wearing blue jeans and driving a pickup truck? Of course it can—depending on the type of property being sold and the prevailing culture in the area. Take an honest look at yourself and ask if what you see is how you want the consumer to see you. Your age and the area in which you work will have an impact on your decisions, but the prevailing question is this: "How do I need to look to come across with the image that I wish to project?"

First impressions. Understand that everything you do communicates something. And first impressions really do count. If an e-mail is not responded to in a reasonable amount of time, an incoming floor call is answered in a distracted manner, or you appear inappropriately dressed when showing property, something is being communicated that may contradict all the professional advertising that you have invested in to attract the real estate consumer. Think about your own impressions when you first met a salesperson or professional in another field. Did you immediately feel a sense of rapport and confidence at the first meeting or were you "turned off" by the person's actions or appearance? Did you ultimately end up working with that person in spite of a weak first impression or did you just walk away? Keeping in mind that there is never a second chance at a first impression, determine exactly what type of image you wish to convey in all of your marketing efforts.

Staying Current

To help build your image as a successful real estate professional, you must constantly collect information on current issues and be willing to adjust your thinking when new or different information arises.

Do you subscribe and listen to local, regional, and national media for consumer trends? Are interest rates rising or going down? Is a local subsidiary of a national company closing its doors? Did you know your local grade school is expanding because of a rise in enrollments? Are same-gender partnerships now being recognized by your local government? Keeping abreast of changes will make you better prepared to adapt your own marketing to evolving markets and consumer trends.

For Example Years ago when the adjustable-rate mortgage (ARM) was first introduced, many real estate professionals immediately jumped to the conclusion that this was a very bad idea and discouraged all of their clients and customers from even considering this type of financing. Over time, the ARM has been found to have an acceptable place in the arsenal of financing options and, in fact, can be a very beneficial program for some borrowers.

Staying In Tune with the Consumer

If the first component of marketing is creating an image, the second is understanding the potential customer. The way you respond to others is an important part of who you are and what you represent. It is important to pay attention to what's going on in the world and how it affects consumers. Wars, terrorism, rising or falling employment—they all affect consumer sentiment about purchasing a home. What are your consumer surveys showing? What have your real estate consumers been saying verbally or nonverbally? What do you and your coworkers think about what's going on in the world, and how it will affect your business?

Brokers who have been in the real estate business for many years have noted that the attitude of the consumer in the real estate market trails about six months behind the actual facts about current conditions.

> **For Example** Sellers often believe their home is worth $200,000 because other houses in the neighborhood went for that amount six months ago. The fact that the market has been in steady decline over the past six months and that the appropriate listing price is more like $175,000 is immaterial to them.

On the other side of the coin, consider buyers who still believe they can offer 10 percent below the list price and ask for $3,000 toward closing costs just because they know someone who did that six months ago and the offer was accepted. The fact that the market in their area has just taken a sudden leap upward due to a severe lack of inventory means little to them. For the consumer, perception is reality. For the real estate professional, reality is based on facts. Staying in tune with consumers means accepting them where they are and then using a combination of facts and figures presented in a professional and knowledgeable manner to bring their level of perception up to what is current reality.

BRANDING

Branding is also important to consider when establishing your image as a competent, ethical real estate professional. Think about it. When was the last time you ordered "a coke" for lunch? Or asked someone to "hand me a Kleenex, please"? Did you put the leftover "coke" back in the "fridge"? Did you remember to "Xerox" a copy of your contract? Coca-Cola, Kleenex, Frigidaire, and Xerox have achieved the ultimate in branding *because they have come to stand for what they represent generically*. The "coke" may in fact have been a Pepsi; the "Kleenex" a Puff, or whatever brand of tissue was on sale at the drugstore this week. The "fridge" could have been a GE or Kelvinator, and the "Xerox" copy could just as well be made on a Canon or Hewlett-Packard! Branding occurs when one particular name, or brand, begins to represent the entire genre of a product or service. REALTOR® has also become a "brand" for a real estate agent, even though not all real estate professionals are members of the National Association of REALTORS®. Buyers and sellers refer to "their realtor" without looking for the ® on the agent's business card.

The Company You Keep

Brokerage firms, especially those belonging to a national franchise, also work hard to establish a certain "branding" of their names. ReMax, Century 21, and ERA all spend a great deal of money on advertising to promote the benefits of working with agents affiliated with these brand-name companies. Just as McDonald's expects every Big Mac to taste the same, no matter where customers buy it, these large franchise companies strive to portray the image that customers will receive the same quality service at any one of their affiliated firms. As you begin to develop your own "brand" image, you must have synergy with the brand image being portrayed by your company.

For Example If a real estate sales agent wishes to specialize in high-end luxury properties, the agent needs to be aligned with a national company that is full service and has national, regional, and local marketing channels that reach the agent's customers.

Another agent who is Internet savvy, who likes to work at home and is willing to work with technology-based relocation clients, might consider working with a virtual-agent brokerage that presents itself as a cutting-edge real estate cyber-brokerage.

Brokerage Types

Below are some examples of brokerage types. When choosing an office to affiliate with, remember that the way each of the brokerage types brands itself should not conflict with your own real estate business branding. Watch for ads from the different types of companies. What "brand" do they seem to be trying to establish? Does it fit with your idea of how you wish to be seen?

Franchise. A franchise brokerage affiliates with a franchise company in exchange for marketing and name recognition; for example, a ReMax or Century 21 office.

National. A national brokerage firm affiliates with a company that provides national marketing and name recognition; for example, Coldwell-Banker or Prudential.

Regional. A regional brokerage firm affiliates with a company that provides regional marketing and name recognition; for example, Long & Foster or Weichert.

Independent. An independent brokerage firm does not affiliate with any other national or regional company. This type of brokerage may range in size from a single office to multiple branch offices.

Auction. An auction brokerage firm holds auctions for sellers to market properties to consumers or businesses.

Builder/developer. A builder/developer brokerage firm focuses primarily on new construction or rehabilitation of existing properties.

Fee for service. This emerging menu-based brokerage format contracts with consumers for specific services that are part of the transaction process at a fixed fee or rate of compensation. A sample menu could include the following:

- Enter home in multiple listing services for a fee of $750
- Host public open house for $100
- Negotiate contract for a fee of $1,000

Discount. Discount brokers market to the consumer by offering a lower commission for listings or transaction services. They appeal to value-driven sellers by offering limited services in exchange for a lower commission or fees. For example, Help-U-Sell is a discount broker.

For sale by owner. These brokerages market directly to sellers selling their own property; offer sellers a variety of property advertising services. They can also include conversion to a fee-for-service brokerage or full-service brokerage.

Buyer representation only. These firms only represent buyers in their market area. Depending on the brokerage agreement, they receive compensation from either the buyer or the seller.

Salaried agents. These licensed real estate sales agents are compensated by their brokers in the form of a salary instead of a straight commission. Some brokerages offer a variation where they pay an additional bonus compensation to the agents when the agents meet predetermined sales goals. Salaried agents are hired with standardization of job description, appearance, transaction management, and work hours.

Internet/e-commerce. An Internet consumer-based brokerage provides the real estate sales agent with sales prospects from the brokerage Web site. Typically the real estate sales agent works from a home office and reports to a regional managing broker.

Commercial. Commercial brokers specialize in forms of commercial properties such as office buildings, shopping centers, multifamily buildings, land development, and businesses.

YOUR PERSONAL BRANDING

Professionalism Is the Key

Real estate sales professionalism involves knowing the market, the transaction process, business ethics, and being the voice of reason in what can be a very emotional process for clients. The client's first impression starts with the first phone conversation or e-mail, or your introduction at the office or open house. Be courteous, tasteful, and respectful. Think seriously about the impact you make. Plan to have a simple classic wardrobe and jewelry, a clean auto, and an organized desk and briefcase.

Opinions differ about the value of other image builders, such as having a picture of yourself on your business card, wearing a name tag, and using a name rider with your picture on your For Sale signs. Keeping foremost in mind how you want to appear to potential clients, go with whatever makes you feel comfortable. The use of cell phones and pagers in the real estate sales world is a given, but when to use them is also a professional issue. When out with clients, it is important for them to feel that they are your number one priority. Distracting cell-phone calls make them feel like just one of your client "pack." If you are expecting a client to call, be proactive and return calls when you have a break. Grouping your calls to be returned is a good professional time management tool.

Professionalism in E-Mail, Faxes, Voice Mail, Snail Mail, and on the Phone

Clients, other real estate sales agents, and transaction-support professionals all need to be communicated with many times during the transaction process. Learning to communicate efficiently with them will give you the advantage of being a real "pro" to work with.

E-mail. E-mail has become an effective form of communication in real estate sales. It's fast, inexpensive, and can be done any time of day. Keep e-mail remarks concise and somewhat formal until your clients have indicated a more relaxed tone is acceptable to them.

For Example Here is an example of a somewhat formal message.

Dear Mr. Harrison,
As per your request of yesterday, I am attaching five listings that appear to be in the price range and location that you and Mrs. Harrison are seeking. Please either call me or notify me by e-mail if 10:00 A.M. on Saturday will be a convenient time for us to look at these properties.

Sincerely,
Rebecca Salesleader

For Example Here is an example of a message in a more relaxed mode.

Hi Jack,
Five listing sheets for you to eye-ball. How about you and Sally meeting me at 10:00 A.M. Saturday and we'll go take a look. E-mail or give me a call—See you soon!

Becky

It is also a good idea to read back over any e-mail message before hitting the send button. Remember that the written word does not have the advantage of inflections or tone of voice. The message may come across as angry, sarcastic, or discouraged. Reading it out loud to yourself will help you set the right tone. It is often helpful to be able to follow the line of conversation through earlier messages, but be careful that the "string" does not become too long and cumbersome. Another caution: if you receive a message that has been sent to multiple receivers and you do not want your response to go out to everyone on the list, be sure to hit "Reply" and not "Reply All."

The new CAN-SPAM Act regulations for the use of e-mail will be discussed in detail in Chapter 5.

Facsimile machine. The real estate sales professional uses the fax machine extensively. You fax contracts, listings, and other supporting documentation to clients, lenders, appraisers, title or escrow companies, etc. Create a professional-looking fax cover sheet with information and numbers specific to you and your brokerage firm in a professional word processing program. Your brokerage office may also have a fax template that you can adapt to your marketing style. Be sure that the date and time stamp that appears at the top of the page is accurate. Sometimes having proof of an exact time and/or day can be critical in contract negotiation.

Regulations similar to those for the Do-Not-Call Registry and under the CAN-SPAM Act are in the process of being finalized and are also discussed in Chapter 5.

General correspondence. You will write many business letters in residential real estate sales. They may be letters for prospecting, agent introduction, press release cover letters, media-kit letters, client thank-you notes, and market analyses prepared for third-party relocation companies. Professional word processing software has a variety of letter templates. Pick a style that fits best with your choice of business branding. Sample letters for a variety of purposes are included in Chapter 4.

Over the telephone. Voice mail and telephone skills are critical to your professional success in real estate. The way you answer the phone and leave greetings and messages conveys an important marketing message to your clients and other real estate sales professionals. Always identify yourself and greet the other party in an energetic, professional manner. People tend to treat you the way you treat them, especially in the virtual world of telephones and e-mail. Return communications as soon as possible. People appreciate a return call, message, or e-mail by the end of the same business day.

PROFESSIONALISM IN PRACTICE

Business ethics in real estate practice is not only good business, it is required by the National Association of REALTORS®. Every four years, members of NAR must complete the required four-hour ethics course to remain in good standing with the national association. Once you hold a real estate license you are perceived to be in a superior knowledge position over the consumer in the real estate transaction. State regulators, arbitration boards, and disciplinary committees expect you to follow and uphold city, county, state, and federal laws along with ethical treatment of all parties involved in the transaction.

You might be confronted at some point in your real estate sales career with clients or other real estate sales agents requesting you to do something that you feel appears to be unethical. Share the situation in confidence with your managing broker and determine what the best course of action is. Do not risk all the time, energy, and expense that you have put in to your new real estate sales business for a short-term gain that could deprive you of the professional reputation you have worked diligently to build.

Suggested Dos and Don'ts for a High Level of Professionalism

Although it might seem that most of these suggestions are merely common sense, it can be helpful to have some professional guidelines, especially for agents just entering the business.

DO

- Dress professionally; your style should reflect your market.
- Treat others as you would like to be treated.
- Allergies are on the rise; avoid being the source of offensive aromas from strong perfumes, colognes, after-shave lotions, and tobacco.
- Listen in an active manner to your clients. Eye contact is important, but staring is unsettling.
- Keep your office organized; you create a first impression in the first seconds clients meet you and see your office.
- Respect other cultures and lifestyles. Fair housing rules real estate sales agents. Think before you talk, it could be an expensive remark!
- Follow up, follow up, and follow up. The biggest consumer complaint about real estate agents is that agents never call back.

- Return phone calls or e-mails in a timely manner (within 24 hours).
- Use breath mints!
- Limit or omit cell-phone use when with clients.
- Answer your phone in a professional manner.
- Respect your client's time.
- Be on time for appointments.
- Adopt a "Customer Is Always Right" philosophy.
- Learn from every situation—every case is different.
- Keep conversations with clients focused.
- Know where you're driving. *Mapquest.com* is great!
- If you need glasses/contacts or hearing aids, wear them.
- Always have a pen and paper.
- Always have business cards.
- Stay calm when your clients are emotional—it may only be a house to you but to them it is a home.
- Drive defensively and focus on the road at all times.
- Know when to talk and when to be silent.
- Listen to client and customer objections. Offer possible solutions. If nothing works, go on to the next property.
- Watch for body language, but be careful. Maybe she is only crossing her arms because she is cold, not shutting you out.

DON'T

- Discuss religion or politics.
- Gossip about your clients, listings, or potential customers.
- Talk on your cell phone while driving clients.
- Let your hair turn off your clients! Drop that dated style or comb-over.
- Use your car as a mobile storage locker. Keep interior and exterior clean and odor free.

- Interrupt your clients.
- Swear or curse.
- Pretend to know about communities or housing styles that you don't actually know about.
- Yell at your clients.
- Become emotional even though clients may be.
- Discriminate. Keep updated on fair housing.
- Over-promise. (Good rule of thumb: Under-promise and Over-produce).
- Lie, cheat, or steal from anyone.
- Eat while talking on the phone.
- Chew gum or smoke when with clients.
- Drink alcoholic beverages when working.

Professional Designations

You can create another type of branding by earning professional designations. Holding a particular designation is an additional marketing tool that creates a unique selling statement because it lets the real estate consumer know that you have received additional real estate certification. Some of the most popular designations are as follows:

Accredited Buyers Representative (ABR). This designation from the Real Estate Agent Council signifies that experienced real estate sales agents have been trained in specifically representing the buyer.

Accredited Land Consultant (ALC). The REALTORS® Land Institute centers this designation on recognized experts in land brokerage transactions of five specialized types: farms and ranches;

undeveloped tracts of land; transitional and development land; subdivision and wholesaling of lots; and site selection and assemblage of land parcels.

Accredited Residential Manager (ARM). This designation is for individuals who manage rental apartment complexes, mobile homes, condominiums, single-family homes, single-room-occupancy apartments, and homeowners' associations, and for individuals who are resident managers, property managers, or asset managers.

Certified Residential Specialist (CRS). The CRS designation recognizes high achievement in sales education and sales experience. All real estate sales agents who want to keep abreast of the latest sales and marketing techniques, enhance their professionalism, and increase their earning power can become certified after completing the required courses and level of production.

E-pro. This training program is presented entirely online to certify real estate agents and brokers as Internet Professionals.

Graduate REALTOR® Institute (GRI). The GRI designation is earned by completing a national program of specialized and advanced education for the licensed real estate sales agent. The program consists of study of special aspects of real estate, such as residential marketing, cost basis, appreciation methods, investment real estate, construction, real estate tax concepts, 1031 tax exchanges, capital gains, and various types of mortgage programs.

Recreation and Resort Specialist (RRS). This new certification is available to experienced real estate sales agents with proof of successful closed transactions plus completion of a two-day core course that focuses on recreation and resort properties.

Seniors Real Estate Specialist (SRES). Real estate sales agents with the SRES designation help senior citizens make wise decisions about selling the family home or obtaining a reverse mortgage, buying rental property, and managing the capital gains and tax implications of owning real estate.

MAINTAINING BRAND LOYALTY

Brand loyalty needs to be continually reestablished in innovative ways. Recall that in the mid-1980s after years of using the same designs on its automobiles, General Motors saw its customers turn to the new Ford Taurus. Ford had studied what General Motors customers were tired of and developed a new product for them. Over the following years, the Taurus took market share from General Motors, as did foreign automakers that offered "new and exciting" models to bored GM customers. Brand loyalty is hard to obtain and even harder to maintain. It takes a concentrated effort to keep providing those brand-loyal consumers with a product that they will continue to enjoy and continue to purchase. You are going to work very hard to develop your brand name—don't become a General Motors and let a Ford take away your business.

> **For Example** Helen Triedandtrue has been the leading real estate agent for almost 15 years in the subdivision where she and her family live. Helen has become an expert in every aspect of living in that community—schools, recreation, safety, shopping, property values, and environmental issues. Helen has truly become the "brand name" for that area. But Susie Startup began a door-to-door "let's get acquainted" campaign shortly after moving into the area. Susie has three children in the local schools serving that area and has included the parents of all of the children in Susie's kids' classrooms on her sphere-of-influence list. Susie attends every school sports event and other activities and is making a real inroad on Helen's "territory."

IN CONCLUSION

Every real estate agent's dream is to have everyone within their acquaintance automatically bring up the agent's name whenever anyone mentions buying, selling, or leasing real estate. Ideally, the agent's name has become "branded" in the practice of real estate. Unfortunately, most people in this country know a number of real estate agents. In order to become the household word for real estate in your area, you must take steps to develop your own "brand." This can be accomplished through your professional appearance and actions. Your brand is reflected in your business card, brochure, advertising, e-mail, and over the telephone. Your sense of ethics and professionalism in your real estate practice are all a part of establishing what your name brand stands for.

Delivering
Your Message

After spending time and money to get licensed to sell real estate, many new real estate agents are surprised to learn that they need to advertise and market themselves and their listings—usually at their own expense. When new agents ask why they need to market themselves, a stock reply is: "No one knows you are available or your listing is on the market if you don't tell them!" New agents do have their listings entered in the MLS along with those of more experienced agents, but is that enough? How does an agent rise to the top in a competitive business? Answer: Only through effective marketing. Without a comprehensive marketing plan for both self-promotion and listed properties, the new agent will be totally overlooked in the crowd of competitors.

TIMING IS EVERYTHING

When companies bring out a new product or service, they spend a considerable amount of time and money to acquaint potential consumers with its features and benefits. The same should be true for the real estate professional. Whether you are a new licensee or an experienced agent entering a new market, you cannot just sit at your desk waiting for the phone to ring. You have to *make* the phone ring by letting potential real estate consumers know that you are available to fill their real estate needs. In other words, you must market *yourself*.

SO, WHAT IS MARKETING?

Marketing is about influencing another person's opinion, habit, or purchase of goods or services. There is often confusion over the meaning of the terms "advertising," "merchandising," and "publicity" as they relate to the general term of "marketing." Each of these terms has its own meaning and can be applied to specific aspects of real estate marketing, as illustrated in the following examples:

- **Marketing:** All aspects of the advertising, merchandising, and selling of goods and services. *Example from the real estate field: an agent's complete marketing plan identifying the goals to be achieved and actions to be taken in the coming year.*
- **Advertising:** Any means by which an organization seeks to influence the thoughts or actions of an individual, usually used to sell a product or to promote good will. *Example from the real estate field: a 30-second radio air-time slot or an open house ad in the local newspaper.*

- **Merchandising:** Promoting the sale of goods and services through advertising and publicity. Think of "merchandising" as a physical attribute of marketing. *Example from the real estate field: a four-color brochure describing the physical features of each model in a new home project.*
- **Publicity:** That part of promotion dealing with efforts to make the public take notice of a person, product, company, etc. *Example from real estate field: public relations article featuring agent's support of Habitat for Humanity project.*

THE IMPACT OF AMERICAN CULTURE ON MARKETING

During the 20th and 21st centuries, the advertising role of marketing increased as American culture embraced first the industrial revolution and then the technology or information age. A large part of the absorption of these two major cultural changes by Americans was accomplished through marketing and its components. A brief overview of the evolution of advertising in this country provides a background that can help today's agents understand the importance of reaching out to the consumer rather than merely extolling the features of the property. Benefit selling is all about answering this question: "What's in it for me?"

A Little History

Both editorially and through advertisements, newspapers began to influence the reader's opinion about ideas and products or services. Also, Sears Roebuck and Company came out with its "dream book"—a catalog where consumers could now see and purchase goods that they might not have even heard of before. You could actually order your new house from the catalog! Sears's famous kit homes that were shipped to the consumer and constructed on site can still be found in older neighborhoods in many cities and suburbs. Sears's concept that "a picture is worth a thousand words" is still very much in evidence in all of modern-day advertising.

With the advent of the personal computer, advertising moved to a much higher level. You no longer had to seek out advertising—it was now being "pushed" at you. Ads began to flow across the top of Web pages or would suddenly pop up on the screen. By the 1990s, message overload began to hit the consumer—ads on buses, shopping bags, shopping carts, and in public rest rooms, ads on buildings, unsolicited ads in your mailbox, and on your computer.

The new advertising medium, the World Wide Web, took off by quantum leaps and some people predicted that it would change advertising and marketing forever. More and more consumers today receive advertising through e-mail, pop-up ads, and links to affiliate programs. In fact, this medium has become so overused that antispam (unsolicited Internet ads) legislation has become necessary. (The latest antispam legislation will be discussed further in Chapter 5.)

The real estate professional and the Web. What is the role of the real estate professional in terms of online, Web-based marketing? Keep in mind that the ability to reach a great many consumers at one time offers countless opportunities for real estate professionals, but they must be careful to conduct their online marketing in a manner that does not antagonize the consumer. While the ability to make changes and update information almost instantaneously is a wonderful marketing tool, it also means that information must be kept up to date by the real estate professional to avoid losing credibility.

ONE SIZE DOES NOT FIT ALL!

The number and frequency of advertising messages being delivered to consumers has become so oversaturated that savvy marketers have had to rethink how to reach consumers. The ability for marketers to differentiate between a "want" and a "need" has become increasingly important. The majority of American consumers today are able to purchase their needs without a great deal of prodding from advertisements, which means that advertising has had to become more focused on meeting the *wants* of the consumer. *The challenge for the advertiser is to make that consumer "want" a particular product, regardless of cost or other considerations.*

Marketers also discovered that members of different target groups view products and their perceived value differently. "One size fits all" just does not work for most products or services. Niche marketing, where one particular group has been selected based on some element of commonality, whether it be ethnicity, religion, age, economic strata, or any other choice of defining a group, speaks directly to the specific wants and needs of that group.

For example, Feng Shui can be an important factor in selecting a new home for some couples. The niche marketer must not only address the need for a home but, more importantly, pay attention to the want side of the equation. The couple *needs* a house, but they *want* one that conforms to the Feng Shui principles. Another example is the senior citizen widow who *needs* a place to live but *wants* one where she will have the companionship of other seniors like herself. Young first-time homebuyers *need* a house they can afford, but they *want* one with potential for expansion in the future. The niche marketer spends a great deal of time analyzing the lifestyle and wants and needs patterns of the members of the selected niche group.

ESTABLISHING A BOND OF COMMONALITY

One primary characteristic of today's marketing environment is the shift from "buy our product" to the more specific "our product is like you, your lifestyle, or special interest." Establishing this bond of commonality makes consumers feel that this is a product or service that provides a benefit for them. The decision to purchase then becomes easier and they are more likely to remain loyal to a particular brand of product.

Once marketers have established a relationship with their consumers, they can begin to pitch other products or services to them based on that relationship. The other products or services related to their core brands are *cross merchandised* based on the existing relationship between the consumer and the original product. This cross merchandising can be taken to another level, where marketers include parallel products or services from other businesses when they sell a product or service.

For Example You order merchandise from a catalog and when your purchase arrives it has an envelope enclosed with "special offers" from other companies. In real estate this cross merchandising could be reduced rates on moving services when you buy or sell a home through XYZ real estate company, or a discount on the settlement attorney's charges. It is always less expensive to market your product or service through an existing consumer relationship than to create a new one.

Thanks to the Internet, leading-edge cross merchandising can be seen in many areas of everyday life. When you order a tent from L.L. Bean, the next time you call they will ask if you liked the tent and if you would be interested in their new camp stove and portable refrigerator. When you order a cookbook from *amazon.com*, you will start receiving multiple ads for cookbooks, recipes, pots and pans, etc. When you use your Safeway discount card to buy groceries, they also build a profile of your likes and dislikes.

NATIONAL PRODUCT MARKETERS ENTER REAL ESTATE BROKERAGE

Marketers of other consumer products, such as automobiles and appliances, have become interested in entering into real estate brokerage in order to take advantage of cross merchandising. They hope to sell their core products to consumers of real estate services. One example is GMAC Real Estate. Its owner is GMAC Home Services whose owner is General Motors Corporation. What was the attraction for General Motors (GM) to buy a real estate company? Homebuyers and sellers could have other General Motors products offered to them. For example, GM could now advertise: "Buy a house through GMAC Real Estate and get special offers on Frigidaire appliances, GM automobiles, etc." GM understood that homes were just one more consumer product that it could use as a way to cross-sell its other products.

Relationship-Based Marketing

Not surprisingly, relationship-based marketing is based on fostering strong and solid relationships. This marketing strategy is the major premise behind niche marketing. In niche marketing an agent develops a sphere of influence of people with whom a relationship has been built. This relationship may be based on common interests through ethnicity, nationality, religion, lifestyle, age, work opportunities, or any one of many other options. The critical point is that the agent has already established a sense of confidence with that person and now is in a position to be trusted with handling a real estate transaction. From the point of view of the consumers, they know that they are working with an agent who best understands their particular needs and wants.

Product Marketing Sets the Foundation for Real Estate Marketing

An understanding of the changes occurring in overall consumer product marketing helps establish a foundation on which to build an agent's ideas for the marketing of real estate. Real estate marketing may be for a product (house, retail store, condominium, rental project), for a brokerage firm, or for an individual agent. A variety of techniques may be used for marketing a property, a company, or a sales practitioner, but an important aspect to the marketing should be the affirmation of the prospective customer.

This customer affirmation is achieved through a shift from emphasizing the "what" that is being marketed to the "who" that is to be the recipient of the message. Careful tracking of responses to that effort makes it possible to determine if the marketing is in fact reaching those to whom it is directed.

TYPES OF MARKETING

There are two basic categories of marketing: institutional and direct marketing. Each serves a different purpose, and, in most cases, both are necessary for a successful real estate business. Whether institutional or direct, the marketing effort will evolve around the four Ps of Marketing:

1. **Product:** What you sell; property, service, idea, or person
2. **Price:** The list price or commission for real estate services
3. **Placement:** Where and when the service or property is presented to real estate consumers. Newspapers, radio, television, magazines, Web sites, floor duty, public open houses, mailings, newsletters, telephone directories, billboards, car signs, business cards, letterhead, and fax cover sheets
4. **Public Relations/Promotion:** The advertising, publicity, public relations, and sales designed to inform and persuade real estate consumers about your product or services

Institutional Marketing

Institutional marketing in real estate promotes the name of a brokerage firm or an individual agent without any reference to specific properties being sold. This type of general marketing does not usually anticipate any type of direct response. It is used to reinforce a brand name with multiple messages in one or more media. Large franchise operations often place ads on television to promote business for their various independently owned companies. An individual agent may also make use of institutional advertising. For example: "Just Listed/Sold" postcards mailed to a general mailing list reinforces the agent's productivity to the card recipient but does not anticipate a direct response.

Customer Referral Marketing

The oldest and least expensive form of marketing is word of mouth. If you hold true to your marketing mission statement, act professionally, timely, and ethically, this highly effective form of marketing will reward you. Ask your customers for testimonials about your business, and ask them for names and permission to contact friends or family members who might have a real estate need. Testimonials let those who actually used your service tell how good their experience was and give evidence to those who want to find out more about you and your quality of service.

Direct Marketing

Direct marketing is an interactive system that uses one or more advertising media to effect a measurable response and/or transaction for a specific geographic location. The results of the direct marketing activity are then stored in a database for future reference and planning. To increase the percentage of response to a direct marketing mailing, the marketer will often enclose a self-addressed and stamped return card. The value of the higher percentage of response must be weighed against the increased cost of the mailing.

The essential element of direct marketing is to determine the target market and then direct all marketing materials to meet the interests of that particular market. A target market may be based on any specific subject. The following represent just a few of the possibilities:

- **Geographic area:** inner city, suburban subdivision, historic area
- **Demographic group:** senior citizens, ethnic group, first-time homebuyers
- **Type of housing:** condominiums, resort property, farm or ranch

Niche Marketing

One special use of the direct market approach is in niche marketing. As stated earlier in this chapter, niche marketing is a marketing strategy that is directed to a specific group of consumers who have a shared interest in common. This shared interest can be based on culture, nationality, age, work experience, or lifestyle.

Some examples of niche markets that can be effectively used in real estate practice are as follows:

- Senior citizens
- Immigrants
- Nationality
- Gender
- Single parent head of household
- Community interest organizations
- Protected classes
- Political groups
- Professional
- Spiritual
- Sexuality
- Military
- International clients

The secret to success in working with a niche market is to either already have an established base of interest within that group or be willing to develop your own knowledge and understanding of the special needs and interests of the group. Niche marketing is based on relationships, not geography. It is natural for people to enjoy working with someone that they know and trust. They are also more likely to refer you to someone else. It takes time and patience to develop a niche market, but it does result in a loyal base of clients.

Business-to-Business Marketing

Marketing directly with letters and phone calls to housing offices at colleges and universities, corporate human resources offices, and other businesses that have a supply of new people relocating into your market is an effective way to build your real estate sales business. Relationships can be built with rental housing offices that will then send referrals of their clients who have decided they would rather purchase than rent (in return for you referring your rental prospects to them). Marketing to other real estate transaction service providers such as attorneys, mortgage brokers, appraisers, and home inspectors is another good source of referral business.

Agent-to-Agent Marketing

Developing a postcard program to market quarterly to other real estate sales agents, regionally or nationally, for their referral business is an effective tool. When attending trade seminars, conferences, and relocation meetings, take the time to meet and develop relationships with other agents outside of your market to build referral business. Within your own market area, develop relationships with other professionals who specialize in other fields of real estate such as commercial, leasing, or farm properties.

PUBLIC RELATIONS/PROMOTION

Public relations—one of the 4 Ps of marketing—deals with how you and your business relate to your community. The two sides of public relations are promotion and publicity. Promotion refers to programs designed to improve the perception of a person, product, or concept. Promotional programs are most likely to be originated by you or by someone you have hired. Publicity is free editorial coverage based on information about you, your company, or your services. Publicity must be factual, interesting, newsworthy, local, and timely. Some examples follow:

- *New Service Publicity:* Informs the consumer of a new feature or benefit of your service.

> **For Example** "Visit our updated Web site that now includes 'Virtual Tours' of featured properties!"

- *Consumer Education:* Informs the consumer of how to better utilize your service, without a direct pitch for a sale.

> **For Example** "On the third Thursday of each month, ABC Real Estate Company offers free first-time homebuyer seminars."

- *Issue Sponsorship:* Shows support of community activity.

> **For Example** "ABC Real Estate Company is proud to sponsor Habitat for Humanity Second Annual Silent Auction and Reception to benefit their land purchase program."

- *Event Sponsorship:* Shows support of special event.

> **For Example** "Martin A. Gent and ABC Real Estate Company are proud to sponsor the first suburban gay and lesbian business and resource expo on February 1, 2004."

Press Release Content

Your public relations/promotion effort will utilize press releases. Here are a few tips to make them stand out. A press release should include a headline, a lead paragraph followed by the who, what, when, where, and why information, followed by supporting text and images, and should close with information about the company and/or person.

Press Release Dos and Don'ts

It helps to establish a track record of well-written, properly prepared press releases. Always be sure to have the most important information in the lead and following paragraphs. Press releases are often shortened to fill in an available slot in the paper and your last few paragraphs may be cut off. Here is a simple list of Dos and Don'ts.

DO

- Follow standard submission format guidelines:
    - double-space the whole release
    - type "more" at the bottom of the page, if is there is a second page included in the release
    - indicate end of release with ### symbols
- Include your name, address, telephone number, and Web site address
- Use an attention-getting headline (something timely or relating to a local issue)
- Make sure it's interesting to the general public (the fact that you attended a national convention is only marginally interesting; your new ability to provide the most up-to-date marketing tools for your listing means much more)
- Follow up on your press release with media contacts
- Remember to include who, what, when, where, and why

DON'T

- Make it too long (three or four paragraphs is usually enough)
- Be late (pay attention to deadlines)
- Be self-promotional (remember, it's all about them)
- Forget to include key information or details (cross-check your facts)
- Make spelling or grammar mistakes
- Forget to include related photos

Press Release Placement

Do you know where your press release goes in your local paper? The appropriate section of the paper is determined by the subject of the release. Submitting the release to the wrong editor will usually result in it never being published.

Most major newspapers have the daily paper divided into several distinct sections. Read over your prepared press release and then decide which section of the paper is most appropriate. Typical newspaper sections include the following:

- **Real Estate:** Ask yourself if your listing is truly unique and interesting to the public; for example, a historic home or hard-to-find waterfront property.
- **Business:** Have you received a real estate business award or achieved a new designation? For example, were you Top Producer for the month or year, or have you earned the Accredited Buyer Agent designation?
- **Home & Garden:** Is a current or past client's home being featured on a garden or house walk? For example, was it among selected homes with extensive azalea plantings or homes featuring backyard koi ponds.
- **Technology:** Did your last buyer make use of advanced technology to buy their home? For example, did they find the home on the Internet and purchase it after only seeing a virtual tour?
- **Events Calendar:** Do you or your brokerage firm donate a portion of your profit to a charity or community activity? For example, did you contribute 10 percent of your commission to your local cancer foundation, or did your company sponsor the local annual Special Olympics program?

- **Education:** Do you have something special planned that would help educate the public? For example, are you hosting a first-time homebuyer seminar or a seminar for potential homesellers interested in retirement communities?

Special Activity Press Release

The press release seen in Figure 2.1 is one used to promote a special activity undertaken by Rebecca Salesleader. Rebecca is making use of technology, awards, local sponsorship, and people's personal interest in their home.

Cover Letter for Special Activity Press Release

Marketers often send a cover letter with their press releases. A sample cover letter Rebecca Salesleader sent with her press release is seen in Figure 2.2.

Preparing a Media Kit

A media kit should always be provided whenever representatives of various media are invited to attend a press conference or event. It is also a courtesy to provide the media kit even if you are only sending information to one newspaper editor. The media kit should be a two-pocket folder that includes the following:

- a news release about you or your services (or clients)
- photographs related to the news release

Figure 2.1 / Sample of Rebecca Salesleader's Press Release

FOR IMMEDIATE RELEASE

Press contact: Rebecca Salesleader, 000-000-0000, rsales@abcrealestate.com

REALITY TV HOME MAKEOVER SHOWS COME TO ANY TOWN!

Any Town, Ohio, April 4, 2005—Rebecca Salesleader with ABC Real Estate is Looking for Local Homeowners Whose Dining Rooms or Home Offices Need a Makeover.

Taking a cue from successful television makeover shows such as "Trading Places" and "Sell This House," Rebecca Salesleader with ABC Real Estate is looking for applicants to participate in a makeover of their dining room or home office.

Ms. Salesleader has partnered with Any Town Home Design and Valley Decorators for four makeovers. The budget per makeover is $500 and will be sponsored by Rebecca Salesleader. Applicants should mail or e-mail two photos of their dining room or home office by May 15th. Her mailing address is: Rebecca Salesleader, ABC Real Estate, 0000 Main St., Any Town, OH 00000, or e-mail rsales@abcrealestate.com.

Successful applicants will have their dining room or home office transformed and featured in the *Any Town Times* article with before and after pictures on Sunday June 6th. Ms. Salesleader will host public open houses at each of the four makeover properties also on Sunday June 6th from 1–4 P.M.

About Rebecca Salesleader
Rebecca Salesleader is affiliated with ABC Real Estate, a locally owned and operated full-service brokerage serving Any Town for over 20 years. Ms. Salesleader was office sales leader for the month of February and is a member of the Presidents Club, whose members have been recognized by ABC Real Estate for superior sales volume. Ms. Salesleader is also involved with the Greater Valley Breast Cancer Project through its annual walk-a-thon. Ms. Salesleader's Internet Web site, rebeccasalesleader.com, won a "Golden Site Award" for 2005 from the Greater Valley Association of REALTORS® for site content and navigation.

###

FIGURE 2.2 / Sample of Rebecca Salesleader's Press Release Cover Letter

ABC Real Estate
0000 Main St.
Any Town, OH 00000

April 4, 2005

Susan Editor
Any Town Times
0000 Elm St.
Any Town, OH 00000

Dear Susan Editor,

Because reality television has impacted American culture, I wanted to bring some of its excitement to Any Town. With so many of our local residents busy with families and work, their homes might be in need of an updating. I have partnered with Any Town Home Design and Valley Decorators to find and complete four makeovers in Any Town of two dining rooms and two home offices, at no cost to the homeowners. What a great opportunity to bring smiles to these people after seeing their own rooms transformed in a weekend. I'm sure their smiles will bring smiles to your readers as well. The attached press release would be of interest to your readers as it touches something we all have in common, our home.

I have also enclosed a media kit that gives you background information on ABC Real Estate and myself. I will follow up with you shortly.

Sincerely,

Rebecca Salesleader

Rebecca Salesleader

Enclosure: Press Release

- a background biography and photo of you
- an overview of your company

All items included in the media kit should be current and include the date. They should be attractively packaged and easy to read. Pictures should always be labeled with the names of those appearing in the picture. Use close-up pictures whenever possible. A picture with too wide an area of coverage is often not suitable for the space available in the newspaper. Be sure to include your contact information on each item included in the kit. There is basically no difference in preparing a media kit for a news item about real estate and a media kit for any other piece of information. The main premise is to provide the information you wish to have presented to the public, along with identifying material about yourself. Your odds of having the article actually printed are much greater if a picture is included.

Self-Promotion Press Release

Whenever you complete a required course for a special designation, you are usually given a sample press release that you can easily adapt to send to your local newspaper. Be sure to include a photo. In the example seen in Figure 2.3, Rebecca Salesleader announces that she has just obtained the Seniors Real Estate Specialist (SRES) designation.

A media kit would be submitted to one or more local papers for the Real Estate Section.

FIGURE 2.3 / Sample Self-Promotion Press Release

FOR IMMEDIATE RELEASE

Press contact: Rebecca Salesleader, 000-000-0000, rsales@abcrealestate.com

LOCAL REALTOR® RECEIVES SRES DESIGNATION

Any Town, Ohio, April 4, 2005—Rebecca Salesleader with ABC Real Estate Achieves Special Designation for Assisting Senior Citizens with Real Estate Transactions.

Recognizing the growing need for agents who specialize in working with the fast-growing population of seniors in Any Town, Rebecca Salesleader recently completed the course offered by the Senior Advantage Real Estate Council®. Completion of this two-day course dealing with seniors' special needs and concerns—reverse mortgages, recent property and estate tax reforms, and probate and living trust issues—has resulted in the awarding of the Senior Real Estate Specialist® designation to Rebecca Salesleader. Seniors Real Estate Specialists (SRESs) throughout the country are helping seniors make decisions about selling the family home, buying rental property, managing capital gains and estate tax, and other important issues.

The formal presentation of the SRES pin and certificate to Salesleader will be made at the quarterly meeting of ABC Real Estate on Wednesday of this week at the Holiday Inn West.

About Rebecca Salesleader
Rebecca Salesleader is affiliated with ABC Real Estate, a locally owned and operated full-service brokerage serving Any Town for over 20 years. Ms. Salesleader was office sales leader for the month of February and is a member of the Presidents Club, whose members have been recognized by ABC Real Estate for superior sales volume. Ms. Salesleader is also involved with the Greater Valley Breast Cancer Project through its annual walk-a-thon. Ms. Salesleader's Internet Web site, rebeccasalesleader.com, won a "Golden Site Award" for 2005 from the Greater Valley Association of REALTORS® for site content and navigation.

###

IN CONCLUSION

A common mistake that is made in all types of selling is the misconception that advertising is all there is to marketing. In fact, marketing includes all aspects of the advertising, merchandising, and public promotion for the sale of goods and services. The changes in advertising during the 20th and 21st centuries reflect the ongoing changes in the American culture through the use of print, radio, TV, and most recently the Internet. The major change has been a gradual shift from the importance of the product to the affirmation of the consumer. The message is no longer "buy this product because it is the best." It is now "buy this product because it is the one best suited to you and your lifestyle."

Ongoing social and lifestyle trends must be considered as part of marketing plans. Institutional marketing is for the general promotion of a company or an agent rather than for specific properties for sale. Direct marketing seeks a response from the consumer for the sale of either product or services. When marketing is specifically directed to a particular group, it is called niche marketing. Niche marketing is more geared to establishing relationships with people than to exploiting any geographic area. Other types of direct marketing include cross merchandising, customer referrals, and business-to-business or agent-to-agent referrals.

Public relations within your community is done by either promotion or publicity. Promotion is generally self-generated with the intent of improving the perception of the agent or company. Publicity may be free and is based on information that is factual and interesting. A well-written and properly prepared press release that is published in the newspaper has the advantage of promoting you in a way that the public perceives as news rather than as advertising.

3

Developing a Marketing Plan

The first objective in preparing a marketing plan is to decide exactly what you plan to market. From the broker/owner point of view, it may be the company itself, the agents affiliated with that office, or properties that the firm has currently listed. For a sales agent, the decision would be whether the marketing is for the agent personally or for properties currently listed by that agent. Once a determination has been made about what exactly is being marketed, then the development of the marketing plan can begin.

THE MARKETING PLAN

Developing a marketing plan is no different from creating any other type of business plan. It is simply a business plan specifically defined for marketing. Your marketing plan may be for either self-promotion or to attract buyers for listed properties. In either case, it is important to follow the necessary steps for development. As with most business planning, there are four important *phases:*

1. Doing the research
2. Developing the plan
3. Implementing the plan
4. Evaluating the results

Each of the four phases is critical to the success of the overall plan and must be completed in the sequence outlined above to be effective. Launching a marketing plan without having completed the necessary research is almost sure to lead to failure.

PHASE 1—DOING THE RESEARCH

Marketing today is often done with a "fire, ready, aim" approach that seldom hits the target! Literally hundreds of thousands of dollars are spent on gigantic marketing efforts with little or no prior research to determine first, if there is a market for this specific product, and second, how best that market can be reached. You can be assured that Budweiser, Pepsi, and other firms that spend 2.3 million dollars for a 30-second slot on Super Bowl Sunday have done their research. They know exactly who their audience is and what is most likely to appeal to them! And how do they know that? By conducting extensive research.

Research Begins at Home

Start your research by taking a good hard look at yourself. Take some time to thoughtfully and honestly answer the following questions:

- What are my special skills?
- What specific education do I have that makes me an expert in a particular area?
- What is it about me that would make people want to work with me?
- What are the benefits the client will receive by signing up with me as either their listing agent or buyer's agent?

Any good marketer will tell you that you have to know your product before you can sell it. Well, you *are* the product you are selling, and you had better know why people should "buy"—or in this case "hire"—you. The consumer wants to know "what's in it for me?" Benefit selling of yourself is just like benefit selling of a product. If Ford tells you that your new car has antilock brakes, you say: "So what?" If Ford tells you that your new antilock brakes will prevent skidding on an icy road and getting hurt, you listen. If you tell consumers that you have the ABR—Accredited Buyer Representation—designation, they politely nod. If you explain that through your additional training in representing buyers you will be in a position to help negotiate the very best deal in the purchase of their new home, you will get their attention. Know your own selling points and be able to present those features as those with perceived value for your potential clients.

Enjoying What You Do

Most of us do those things best that we enjoy doing. There is no reason that you cannot focus your real estate career in an area that provides you with the most enjoyment. Many times new agents will chastise themselves for not being a good listing agent. Pressured by brokers and fellow agents, they have it drilled into them that for good agents to succeed they must have multiple listings.

Unfortunately, they absolutely hate the whole listing process; at least everything that comes after the euphoria of obtaining it. If this is you, don't try to market yourself as a top-notch listing agent! Try answering the following self-test on listing agent activities:

AGENT ACTIVITY	YES	NO
I like preparing a comparative market analysis.	❏	❏
I enjoy assembling an attractive listing presentation book.	❏	❏
I am happy to meet with prospective sellers.	❏	❏
I welcome the chance to prepare a home for showing.	❏	❏
I find pricing a home an exciting challenge.	❏	❏
It's always a pleasure to hold an open house.	❏	❏

If you answered "no" more than once or twice, it would seem that listings are not your favorite way to practice real estate. On the other hand, some folks absolutely abhor the thought of driving a couple plus their two kids around looking at houses all day Saturday, especially when the four-year-old is sitting in the back seat of your brand new Camry with a purple lollipop in hand! If this sounds like you, forget about marketing yourself as the ultimate buyer agent. We all do a better job if we like what we are doing. Sure, it's never going to be 100 percent pleasure all day every day, but at least the odds become greater for more satisfaction—and better service to the client—if you can spend the majority of your time doing what you enjoy most.

Finding a Match

Once you have determined who you are, what you have to offer, and what area you would like to work in, then start searching for a good match for your skills that you can market to the public. Want to work those foreclosures? Check the HUD and VA lists in the paper, meet with someone at the local office, and take every course available on the subject. Then you will be able to honestly market yourself as an expert on government foreclosed properties. Expand that knowledge further to working with bank foreclosures by meeting with the real estate owned (REO) officer at local banks, search the MLS for bank-owned listed properties, and talk to agents already working with the banks. Once you are secure in your new knowledge, you are ready to market yourself to the public as an expert in working with foreclosure sales. You can also market yourself to the banks as someone knowledgeable in handling such listings.

Would you like to concentrate on listing and selling those upper-scale properties located on the classy side of town? Check the MLS listings and new home subdivisions every day to learn everything you can about what is on the market and what has sold. Locate the agents who are working that area, visit open houses, and preview properties for sale to get a feel for the type of marketing that is going on. What sort of brochures are the current listing agents preparing for these homes? Could you do a more attractive piece? What types of ads are being run? Could you make them more interesting? How was the open house handled? Could you do it more attractively? What other type of marketing techniques are being used? What other creative ideas can you come up with? Do your research and then develop a marketing plan guaranteed to impress these potential clients.

Want to develop your niche working with first-time homebuyers? Entry level homes at affordable prices are hard to find in many areas. You will need to spend time checking newspaper ads, new home projects, and, most important, your own MLS listings every day. Drive around your town or city, looking for areas where affordable homes may still exist. Sometimes there may only be one or two houses sandwiched in between larger, more expensive homes. Take time to meet with local nonprofit housing groups to see if they have houses in their own inventory that might be available, or if they have down payment assistance programs. Check out your local city housing office for information on any special programs for financial assistance for first-time homebuyers. Watch the paper for estate sales or sales by owners. These properties may not show up in the MLS if they are not actually listed with a broker, but in many cases they are willing to pay a buyer agent's commission. Learn how to negotiate a lease-purchase contract for those who do not quite have the cash they will need to close today, but who will be ready within the next year. And, probably the most important research of all: spend time with several local lenders to learn about the various low down payment programs that are available today.

Do Your Homework First

Remember the smart real estate professional needs to be just as careful as Ford and Pepsi before spending both time and money on marketing. In the following three examples, you can see what happened when three agents developed a marketing plan but neglected to do their research homework!

Example 1—Promoting personal expertise. Let's see what happens to Carlos as a consequence of omitting the research phase. Carlos took all of the courses offered by both the Federal Housing Administration (FHA) and the Department of Veterans Affairs (DVA) and has now decided to market himself as an expert on handling the sale of FHA and VA foreclosed properties. His first marketing action is to place a four inch by four inch ad to run daily in the local newspaper emphasizing the benefits of working with

"Carlos, your FHA/VA foreclosure expert." No matter what this ad may cost, Carlos is confident that it will be well worth it as soon as his first FHA or VA foreclosure sale is completed. After all, isn't everybody looking for a "good deal"? Good thinking, but suppose there were no HUD or VA foreclosed properties for sale in Carlos' immediate market area? Carlos should have done some research! He should have contacted both the local FHA and VA offices in his city. They could have provided him with specific information on the number, location, and price for all government foreclosed houses in the area. He should also have been watching the daily newspapers for advertisements for HUD and VA foreclosed properties. By doing his research first, Carlos would have seen that there really was no need for a HUD/VA foreclosure expert in his market area.

Example 2—Promoting name recognition. Another example of neglecting research is 23-year-old Sally Graham. Sally recently graduated from college with a bachelor's degree in real estate. She is confident that her age, along with her outside interests and hobbies, will allow her to become the area expert in working with first-time homebuyers. Her first goal for marketing herself is to send out a 1,000-piece "personal touch" letter offering her new expertise and services to the neighborhood where she grew up. Her idea of achieving some benefit from name recognition—her family has lived in and been active in community activities in that neighborhood for three generations—is a good one. Political campaign consultants say that 85 percent of success at the election polls is based on name recognition. Wouldn't this strategy work for her? Actually, probably not. She may have a name that is well-known in the part of town where she plans to target her mailing, but here is the catch: because her parents are now in their 50s, so are many of their neighbors. And some are actually closer to age 70. These are obviously not typical first-time homebuyers themselves, although possibly they will have children or grandchildren who might be interested in her services. A second problem is that property in the area where she grew up has appreciated greatly in price, with most homes now well over the $300,000 mark. Sally is totally missing her market. She has just spent a lot of time gathering names and addresses, preparing her mailing, and paying to have it sent out but with prospects for only a minimal return.

Sally needed to do her homework first! Sally could have pulled up demographic statistics from the U.S. Census Bureau (*http://www.census.gov*). She could have talked to her parents about the number of young, middle-aged, or elderly people that seem to live in the neighborhood now. She could have pulled tax records for the adjacent neighborhoods that would have given her an overall idea of the value of properties in the neighborhood. She could have printed out at least the most recent months of sales data from her local multiple-listing system to provide her with current information on properties listed for sale and those that have closed. Accumulating the results of this data gathering would have shown her that her old neighborhood was way overpriced for a first-time homebuyer market. Her time and efforts could be spent more profitably in a different area.

Example 3—Promoting special skills. In addition to marketing an area of expertise, agents may also wish to market themselves by promoting other special skills, such as proficiency in another language or knowledge of the culture and special interests of a particular group. For example, Mai Ling is a computer expert of Chinese-American background who lost her job with a dot.com company last year and decided to prepare for a new career in real estate. Mai Ling is proficient in both Mandarin and Cantonese and has a good understanding of the Feng Shui principles that are important to many buyers. She has been told that she could do very well by concentrating on working with members of the local Chinese community. Unfortunately, she forgot to take this into consideration when she was selecting a brokerage firm with which to affiliate. She ended up signing on with the firm that had the largest and most plush offices in a very expensive part of the city. She was attracted by the average house price of the company's listings and, admittedly, she was impressed by the luxurious office and the well-dressed, apparently knowledgeable agents who worked there. The company provided her with elegant introductory note cards, which she promptly sent out to all of her acquaintances both within the Chinese community and outside it. Not too surprisingly, she had very little return. For the non-Chinese recipients of her message, she was considered to be too young and inexperienced. She was competing with the very same agents that she had been so impressed with in the first place. For the more obvious target—those in the Chinese community—her office was inconveniently located on the other side of town and was perceived as being totally "anglicized." In other words, many members of the Chinese community felt that they would not really be welcomed or comfortable in that office atmosphere.

Mai Ling's mistake was neglecting to match her special skills with the appropriate setting. She should have canvassed members of the Chinese community to see whether they felt it would be beneficial to work with an agent who was fluent in Chinese. Next, she should have asked them how far they would be willing to travel to find such an agent. Would they be willing to go across town? Would they feel intimidated by a large, predominantly Caucasian office? Would they be more likely to work with someone located in an office that was more convenient to their home and work? With a little more research and by adhering to the "look before you leap" caveat, Mai Ling would have realized that an office located in the middle of the Chinese community where she would stand out as a expert with her special skills and knowledge would have proven to be a far better choice.

Mai Ling will also need to advertise in English publications to avoid any suggestion of "steering"—a violation of fair housing law.

Researching the competition. Another point to consider in your research involves gauging the amount of competition for clients that currently exists in your chosen field. If there are already two or three agents specializing in foreclosures in your town, you might do better to select a different area of expertise. On the other hand, the fact that one or two agents appear to have all the listings and sales in a certain geographic area "sewn up" should never discourage you from launching your own marketing initiative. A different face with new, creative ideas and a well-thought-out marketing plan can often overtake the existing "experts" already in the field. However, you should never underestimate the competition. They are successful for a reason, and there is probably much you can learn from them. Visit their open houses, watch for their ads in the newspaper and magazines, and observe them in the office whenever possible. See what you find the most attractive about their marketing methods. Look for some element that may be being overlooked and then develop your own special "hook" to attract new clients.

The old adage of "location, location, location" may be valid for determining the value of a property but, remember, there is no substitute for "research, research, research" when developing any type of business planning—especially for a marketing plan.

PHASE 2—DEVELOPING THE PLAN

When your research is complete, you are ready to actually prepare your marketing plan. Depending on whether you are marketing yourself or marketing one of your listings, the actual details will
be different, but the overall concept of developing the plan is the
same. There are four major steps to developing any type of plan:

1. Determine the **purpose** or **mission**
2. Establish the **goals** to be set in order to achieve the purpose
3. Outline the **actions** to be taken to accomplish the goals
4. List the **details** involved in order to carry out each of the
   actions

One further consideration is budget. An elaborate plan that
would cost ten times your available funds is pointless. Marketing
"how-to" books often recommend that 10 percent of your income
should be spent on marketing, and many brokerage firms use this
10 percent figure to set up an office advertising budget. This may
be adequate for maintaining an already established position in the
marketplace but for an agent just getting started, or for someone
attempting to break into a new area, this is probably not adequate.
Also, trying to set an exact percentage of income to be spent on
each marketed listing is not practical because some listings will
inevitably require more marketing than others.

For example, one listing might sell in three days with a total
expenditure of $120 for marketing. Another listing may take nine
months to sell with costs of over $1,000.

A marketing budget should be established that will cover the
total cost for the year for marketing of both yourself and all of your
listings. A more realistic way to budget would be:

Anticipated income: $60,000

Projected marketing budget: $6,000

Keep in mind that this 10 percent figure will not be enough for a new agent or one who is entering into a new area of business or a different market. Typically, new or start-up businesses use 15 percent to 22 percent of their income toward marketing expenses.

Things to consider in preparing your marketing budget. You may find that you will not need to spend money on all of the items listed below in every year's budget, but let this list serve as a reminder of the various categories to be considered. Costs such as designing business cards, brochures, etc., are usually a one-time expense, except for occasional updating. Other expenses like postage, Web hosting, and your e-mail account will occur on a monthly basis.

- Design and printing costs for business cards, personal brochures, Web site, and direct mail
- Photography and development expense
- Copywriter's fee
- Desktop design and publishing software
- High-speed printer to generate proofs or final copies
- Mailing list rentals
- Postage
- Mailing costs, including stuffing, sealing, and sorting
- Advertising space costs, for ads run in various publications
- Monthly rental fee for Web hosting
- Web designer's fees or Web design software
- Webmaster or Web maintenance costs
- Business specific e-mail account
- Customer appreciation and giveaways, holiday calendars, etc.
- Contribution to charity or other community events

Step 1 of Developing the Plan—Determining the Purpose

Step one of developing your plan is set a **purpose,** or some people like to think of it as a **mission.** In some cases the purpose may be to promote yourself as an agent; in others, the purpose is to bring your listing to the attention of the public in hopes of finding a buyer.

Getting your name out there. The purpose for a marketing plan for self-promotion is to make your name known within your local marketplace. Determine whether you have a special skill or ability that you wish to promote. Back up your claim with credentials, success stories, and satisfied client testimonials. Here are some ideas:

- Promote your ability as an expert buyer's agent in a specific area of real estate such as first-time homebuyers, special ethnic groups, second homes, seniors, foreclosures, or any other of the many choices available for establishing a niche market.
- Illustrate your expertise in "staging" a home for better presentation, proper pricing techniques, and effective marketing ideas to attract listing clients.
- Achieve recognition for your top producer status in your local area or as the #1 agent in sales in your office or in your local REALTOR® association.

The important thing is to determine the stated purpose for the marketing plan. Then you are able to "ready, aim, *fire!*" with much better chance of successfully hitting the target!

Setting the purpose for a marketing plan for a listing. The primary purpose for marketing a listing is to bring that particular property to the attention of the marketplace. A secondary purpose could be to provide name recognition for the listing agent in a particular community or for a particular type of property. A third option would be to attract other homeowners that may be considering selling their home. Being able to achieve more than one goal through the marketing for a listing is extremely cost-effective.

Step 2 of Developing the Plan—Establishing Goals

Once the purpose has been determined, whether for self-promotion or for selling a listing, you are ready for Step Two of Developing the Plan, which is to establish **goals.**

Practically everyone has taken numerous courses or seminars focusing on the topic of "goal setting." In most cases, the guidelines are pretty much the same: set the goals, write them down, etc. And that is about as far as most goal setting ever gets. Is it any wonder that goals are seldom reached? Whether your goals are in your personal life, your annual business plan, or your marketing plan, they all share this in common: they should be specific, realistic, obtainable, and measurable.

Setting a realistic goal. You have decided that your purpose for this plan is to market yourself as a first-time homeowner expert. Now you are setting your goals, and the first one is: "I will contact more potential first-time homebuyers." Good idea–lousy goal.

First, you must make this goal *specific:* "I plan to have my name in front of at least 1,000 prospective first-time homebuyers each month."

Next, determine if this plan to reach 1,000 prospects a month is *realistic.* The answer may be "yes," through the use of mailings and other print media. On the other hand, the answer may be "no," if you are talking about face-to-face contacts.

Is this goal *obtainable?* Yes, it is definitely, physically obtainable. There are numerous sources for printing and sending mailings and plenty of print media sites available. The only question would be whether you have either the financial or personal resources to carry out the plan. If not, then you may need to cut the goal back to a number that *is* obtainable.

Is this goal *measurable?* Yes, but you must track your results. You need to keep careful records showing the source of each incoming call or other response to your mailing. Further tracking will show the outcome of each response. Did it result in a new client? Did it lead to a sale? Was there a commission earned? How much total income did you receive from this 1,000-piece marketing effort?

When you initially start making goals, just write down every idea you can. Then go back over the list. You may decide to discard some. Others could be combined or altered slightly. You should end up with a list of four to six goals that will lead you to achieving your stated purpose. Next, take each of those goals and test them against the given benchmarks stated above: the goal must be specific, realistic, obtainable, and measurable. Once you have done this, you will have a list of true *goals,* not just pipe dreams. But these goals will never be accomplished without taking some action.

Step 3 of Developing the Plan—Outline the Actions

The next step is deciding what **actions** must be taken to achieve the goal or goals. Wishful thinking will not work. Each goal should have at least three or four specific actions listed that are directly related to making that particular goal work. If one action seems to be moving in a different direction from the others, it should probably be changed into another goal, with its own set of actions.

Each of the actions developed to achieve the goal must also include a deadline for completion, the designated person responsible for carrying out the action, and a projected budget. In most cases the agent alone will carry out all of the actions, but many agents today do have assistants or may be outsourcing some of the work.

Example of Action Outline

Stated Purpose: Develop reputation as top listing agent in Westbrook Acres.

Goal #1: Obtain a buyer for my listing at 1234 West Avenue in the next 60 days.

Is the goal specific? Yes. Is it realistic? Yes. Is it obtainable? Yes. Is it measurable? Yes. Now list the actions necessary to reach this goal.

ACTIONS	COST	DEADLINE	PERSON RESPONSIBLE
1. Place ad in the local homes magazine	$40	Wednesday	Me
2. Arrange for open house with sellers	$25	Thursday	Me
3. Send invitation to open house to 100 neighbors	$50	Wednesday	Me
4. Place open house in Sunday newspaper	$80	Thursday	Secretary

Step 4 of Developing the Plan—Compile List of Details

The devil is in the details. The action plan described above looks pretty good on paper, doesn't it? But these actions will never happen without careful attention to **detail**. The person who coined the phrase "the devil is in the details" must have been someone who had many plans fail. For every action that is part of a goal there will be numerous details that must be taken care of in order to complete the action. In fact, some items on the detail list may require an additional list of subdetails.

Example of action plus details. If we examine the proposed goal of "getting my name in front of at least 1,000 prospective first-time homebuyers each month," here is a detailed plan for how one agent, working alone, can carry out the action. A list of necessary details is shown under each action:

- **Action:** Run an ad in a local paper or in a homes magazine that is heavily distributed in an area that has many apartment complexes. (Research will have already been done to determine where these areas are located and what paper or magazine is distributed there and what cost is involved.)

Details	Deadline
1. Take picture for ad	Saturday
2. Write the ad and have reviewed by broker	Monday
3. Submit ad to run on Thursday and Saturday next week	Tuesday

4. Prepare a tracking sheet to collect　　　Wednesday
   information from persons responding
   to the ad

Be sure to keep track of all business resulting as a response
to this ad. This will provide a way to gauge the effectiveness
of different ads used during the year.

Expected cost: $80 × 2 = $160 per week

- **Action:** Volunteer to give a first-time homebuyers seminar at
  a local library, church, school, or local place of employment.

Details	*Week 1*
1. Make calls to possible venues to check on availability and cost; arrange for time and date	Monday
2. Visit site to check on room set-up, audio-visual equipment, parking, ability to serve refreshments	Wednesday
3. Develop agenda and make arrangements for guest speakers	Thursday
	Week 2
4. Prepare and place ads for seminar	Tuesday
5. Prepare handout materials	Thursday
6. Be on-site an hour early to check audio-visual equipment, meet guest speakers, greet attendees	Saturday

Expected cost: $150 for site + $50 for refreshments = $200

■ **Action:** Arrange with the broker to hold first-time home-buyer seminars at the office twice a month.

Details	*Deadline*
1. Set up meeting with broker	Tuesday
2. Select days and times for seminars	Tuesday
3. Have events placed on company calendar	Tuesday
4. Prepare ads for local newspaper	Wednesday
5. Prepare sign-in sheets with name, address, and phone numbers for follow-up	Wednesday

Keep careful records of follow-up calls and resulting business. It will be important at the end of the year to see how much new business resulted from these homebuyer seminars.

Expected cost: Broker to pay for ads; $50 for refreshments = $50

Example. Joe Green obtained a new listing on Sunday that he is very proud of, but he realizes that it may be difficult to bring it to the attention of prospective purchasers. The property includes five acres of open land plus a lovely 75-year-old Colonial style house. The house is not old enough to have historic value. It does, however, have many of the charming details that are seldom found today, such as four marble-faced fireplaces, chair rail and crown moldings throughout the first level, wide-panel hardwood floors, and lovely crystal chandeliers in the dining room and foyer. There are four spacious bedrooms on the second level plus a walk-up attic with room for further expansion. On the down-side, there is only one bath on the second level, and the kitchen and bath are both very outdated. At the listing price that is satisfactory to the sellers, Green knows that a simple entry in the MLS will not attract much attention. Too many people would automatically overlook any listing with four bedrooms and only one bath.

Action plan plus details for marketing Green's listing. Green's goal is to find a buyer for the house. Green works alone and will be responsible for carrying out all of the actions. His action plan might look like this:

■ **Action:** Enter listing in multiple listing service

Details	*Deadline*
1. Emphasize special custom features of the house	Monday
2. Suggest possibilities for use of the large yard	Monday

Expected cost: none

■ **Action:** Submit article and picture for Sunday's Featured Homes Section

Details	*Deadline*
1. Take picture suitable for ad, flyers, and other media	Tuesday
2. Submit article and picture to featured homes editor	Wednesday

Expected cost: none if it appears as feature article

■ **Action:** Submit ad with picture for Sunday Open House section in newspaper

Details	*Deadline*
1. Collect additional details from seller about custom features; i.e., his grandfather was the mason who built the fireplace and the fountain down at City Hall	Monday
2. Prepare ad copy stressing custom features and large yard	Wednesday
3. Brainstorm possible uses for large yard; i.e., horses, dog kennel, orchard, flower or vegetable garden, koi pond, swimming pool, tennis court—use your imagination	Wednesday
4. Submit ad copy with same picture from feature article	Thursday

Expected cost: $120

■ **Action:** Submit full-page ad to local homes magazine

Details	*Deadline*
1. Arrange time and day with seller to take photos	Monday
2. Take additional exterior shots of yard	Tuesday
3. Take several interior shots of special features	Tuesday
4. Write ad copy stressing custom features	Thursday
5. Arrange for pickup or delivery of material to magazine	Thursday

Expected cost: $130

■ **Action:** Prepare open house invitation

Details   *Deadline*

1. Use same picture and copy as used in   Wednesday
   newspaper ad
2. Send invitation to homes in nearby   Wednesday
   housing development that has mainly
   three-bedroom homes with very
   small yards
3. Deliver invitation to homes close to   Saturday
   property for sale

Expected cost: $75 preparation and mailing, $25 if delivered

■ **Action:** Arrange for an open house on Sunday

Details   *Deadline*

1. Clear time and day with seller; request   Monday
   they stay away
2. Collect open house directional signs for   Saturday
   placement from main road into property
3. Prepare refreshments and fresh flowers   Saturday
4. Attach balloons or streamers to   Sunday
   directional signs
5. Place directional signs on roads leading   Sunday
   to property

Expected cost: $100

Based on his past experience of working with families, Green believes that this house will appeal most to a couple with young or teenage children whose parents have fond memories of "grandma's house." The property may be too isolated for families with one-year-olds to five-year-olds, have too many stairs for the elderly, and be too much trouble for "dinks" (double-income, no kids). He will concentrate his marketing strategy on areas where target families may be found; i.e., local elementary, middle, and high schools, churches, libraries, soccer fields, ice cream parlors, karate schools, dance studios, and shopping malls.

Green can use the same general picture and copy that he used for his open house invitations and ads to prepare flyers that he can hand out at his targeted locations. Of course, he must always obtain permission. Another action would be to mail the flyer to communities that are a logical target for a "move-up." Statistics show that most people move up to a property about half again as expensive as the one they presently live in; i.e., sellers of $150,000 properties move up to those costing around $225,000; $200,000 owners move up to $300,000, and so forth.

Consulting the experts. Because Green realizes that he is much more familiar with selling new homes, or townhouses in the city, he decides to seek some advice from John D. John has been an agent in Green's office for almost 20 years and has listed many older homes that needed everything from a little TLC to major renovation. In fact, John often buys an old property himself and then renovates it to make it more appealing to today's buyers. John gave Green suggestions for several actions that he can take that will provide him with information that will help him answer questions and respond to objectives from potential purchasers.

John's suggestions. John recommended Green do the following four things:

1. Contact a local builder to obtain an estimate for adding a second bathroom on the second level, and possibly a powder room on the first level. Have plans and estimates available to counter this anticipated objection.
2. Obtain rough estimates from Lowes and/or Home Depot for renovating the kitchen and have brochures and cost information available.
3. Contact a local landscaper for ideas for improvements to the front yard and surrounding open land. Have plans and cost estimates available.
4. Encourage the seller to pay for a thorough home inspection of the house. Identifying and correcting problems beforehand can save a great deal of stress later by limiting the number of defects or deficiencies that might be noted by a home inspector hired by the purchaser.

Green can then sit down with the seller and discuss the possibility of spending money now to correct some of the problems resulting from the home inspection. Dollars spent on improvements prior to selling will often result in a much quicker sale at a higher price.

Put the marketing plan in writing. Each goal in the marketing plan needs to be written down along with its planned actions and outline of details. When you try to carry around your "to do" list in your head, you usually end up going over and over the same things. You are constantly reminding yourself "Don't forget to do this," and "Be sure to have this ready." This creates something like a "squirrel cage" in your brain with your thoughts revolving around the wheel. Committing tasks to a written list provides a great psychological benefit. As the actions are completed, they can be checked off. In effect, this ejects them from the squirreling-mind cycle and frees up your mind to concentrate on other things.

The marketing plan is complete. At this point you should have completed all four steps in developing your plan:

1. Determine the **purpose**, or **mission**
2. Establish the **goals** to be set in order to achieve the purpose
3. Outline the **actions** to be taken to accomplish the goals
4. List the **details** involved in order to carry out each of the actions

You are now ready to move on to Phase 3 of the overall marketing plan.

PHASE 3—IMPLEMENTING THE PLAN

As a familiar advertiser says, "Just do it!" Once the purpose is defined and the goals are established, it is simply a matter of implementing the stated actions complete with details. In other words, you "work the plan." Occasionally you may find that carrying out a particular action is no longer feasible, exceeds the budget, or cannot be completed by the designated deadline. A marketing plan must always have flexibility and the ability to adapt to changing or evolving circumstances.

Track Results as Well as Actions

In addition to carefully tracking the progress for completion of actions, you should also develop a system for keeping track of the results. It is much easier to keep track as you go along, rather than trying to look back at the end of the year to measure the amount and quality of business derived from different marketing efforts. You have seen tracking results included as part of some of the action plans described above. For example, in the action plan for presenting homebuyer seminars, the importance of keeping track of follow-up calls and any resulting sales from those attending the seminar was stressed. It is also important to keep a record of the number of responses from the ads in addition to the actual number of attendees at each seminar.

Be sure to check with all new prospects to find out what aspect of your marketing caught their attention. Did they come to you as a result of an ad in the newspaper, magazine, or radio? Did they meet you at an open house or were they referred to you from someone on your sphere-of-influence list or by a satisfied former client? The rest is just a matter of numbers. Count how many prospects came from each type of marketing; how many prospects became clients; and how many clients actually resulted in sales.

PHASE 4—EVALUATING THE RESULTS

Good tracking records are important because they allow you to evaluate the results. Evaluation is critical in determining the cost effectiveness of each element of the marketing plan. For instance, if it cost $400 to run an ad in a major city newspaper, and that ad resulted in two responses, while it cost $80 to place an ad in the local paper that resulted in four prospects, the value of each ad is obvious.

If the seminar at the local library cost $200 to put on and resulted in four prospects, and the seminar held at the office cost only $50 and resulted in one prospect, the cost factor may not be the only consideration. On the one hand, the importance of having your name associated with an activity presented in a community setting rather than a real estate office may be a significant factor. On the other hand, bringing the prospective purchasers into the office on a low-key, nonpressure basis can create a comfort level for some prospects.

Tracking Systems

To make your contact history and tracking easier, you can purchase computer software programs that are already set up for you. Consider ACT! Contact Software (*www.act.com*) and Data Village (*www.datavillage.com*). Top Producer®, another computer program popular with agents for many years, is completely Internet-based and includes many features to assist you with the tracking process (*www.topproducer.com*).

Keep in mind that you can also develop your own tracking system using Microsoft (MS) Excel spreadsheets. You set up the sheet by designating each column as a different marketing tool, then make entries in the correct column after you ask your prospects what specifically caused them to contact you. You will have columns for Newspaper/Classified, Newspaper/Open House, Radio, Cable TV, Homes Magazine, Open House, Homebuyer Seminar, and all other strategies you are currently using. Review these numbers at the end of each quarter to see what seems to be working best for you.

An even more sophisticated way to use the MS Excel spreadsheet is to track by "key codes." Key codes are commonly used in the advertising world to track direct response from a marketing piece. The key code is entered on the return response mailer or at the bottom of a newspaper ad. When a response is received from either the mailer card or the ad, you make an entry on the MS Excel spreadsheet as to which key code is indicated. The key code on an invitation for a homebuyer seminar mailer might read 01/04HSLib. The bottom of an ad might read 10/04LDChTrib. The code letters will identify the piece to you.

Even the old-fashioned spreadsheets that come on big green pads that you fill in by hand will work. The objective simply is to devise a way to keep track of every prospect, how they came to you, and what resulted from that contact. The level of sophistication that you select for your tracking system will probably depend on how familiar you are with computer programs and the amount of business you normally conduct each year. Whatever system you decide to use, it must be one that you will use faithfully. Trying to remember what people said and catch up at the end of the month will never work. Make your system one that you can and *will* use.

Never think that you do not have enough business to warrant setting up a tracking system. It is much easier to set up a system when your practice is smaller. Have the system in place to handle 20 clients per year and the same system will easily expand to handle 200.

Using the Results

Careful tracking is the only way to calculate the cost effectiveness and end results of your different marketing strategies. The effectiveness of each marketing activity should be measured by the amount of resulting business and also the benefit of establishing name recognition within the community. By the end of the year, it will be graphically clear which of your marketing tools and strategies works best for you. Although you always want to try out new ideas from time to time, it also makes perfect sense to continue with and improve on doing those things that bring you the most results.

Evaluation of the current year's results will help you develop your marketing plan for the following year. If you are obtaining the best results from ads in the homes magazine, perhaps buying an additional page there each month would be good. If most of your prospects come from your open houses, set aside more Saturdays or Sundays for this activity. If the majority of your first-time homebuyer prospects came from the homebuyer seminars that you presented at your office, forget about spending extra dollars to rent the community hall. If you love working with the computer and most of your responses came from e-mail advertising, do more of that and quit forcing yourself to hold open houses. As stated earlier, you do *best* what you like to do. Just do more of it for increased results!

IN CONCLUSION

Once it has been determined exactly what is to be marketed, the marketing plan is then developed through four phases: doing the research, developing the plan, implementing the plan, and evaluating the results. While each of the phases is equally important, the one most often overlooked is research. Developing the plan follows four easy steps: determine the purpose or mission, establish the goals, develop the actions to meet those goals, and list the details in writing necessary to accomplish the actions.

If one marketing action does not seem to work, try something else. Your marketing plan needs to be evaluated regularly as the year progresses but especially at the end of the year. At this point it will become obvious which ideas work best in different situations.

Based on this information, it becomes easier to develop a marketing plan for the next year. But always be open to new ideas and new actions. Doing the same old thing will always produce the same old results. Be flexible, be creative, and be successful!

4

Marketing Tools and Techniques

The primary purpose of all marketing strategies is to deliver a message to the consumer. The message may be an attempt to sell a specific product, to promote a specific brand, or to introduce the consumer to a company with something to sell. In the real estate business we may be "selling" ourselves, our expertise, or our product. Our products are the properties that owners have listed with us in the hopes of getting them sold.

VISUAL-AUDITORY-KINESTHETIC (V-A-K) CUES

In order to better prepare the marketing message, we must first understand something about the psychology of the consumer. Neurolinguistic programming (NLP) is a communication technique that was developed in the 1970s by mathematician John Grinder and linguist Richard Bandler. This technique was designed to help people and companies increase their rate of success through more effective communication. NLP identifies the following three ways in which people process the information that they receive:

1. Visually (V)
2. Auditorily (A)
3. Kinesthetically (K)

The visual process takes place through the eyes and is most affected by pictures and words that relate to seeing. Auditory processing relies more on sound and is affected most by things that are heard or words that relate to hearing. Kinesthetics refers to touching or feelings. The feelings may be internal ones such as joy, fear, comfort, or anxiety. External feelings relate to taste, touch, smell, or physical movement. Words that support such feelings capture the attention of the kinesthetic processor.

Using V-A-K in Marketing

The visual-auditory-kinesthetic (V-A-K) theory was not specifically developed for writing real estate ads, but it can be a useful tool when preparing any type of marketing piece. By using visual words, you are able to attract the interest of the person who processes incoming information through their eyes. By using auditory words, you can catch the attention of the auditory person who processes information by hearing. And with the use of well-placed kinesthetic words, you can establish instant rapport with the person who relies on touch and feelings.

Which Are You—V, A, or K? For a simple test to see which way you process information, answer the following question. When you purchased your new DVD player and tried to hook it up, did you

- carefully read the instruction booklet,
- call up your electronic whiz brother-in-law and ask him to talk you through it, or
- just start plugging in connections and then wait to see what happens next?

Are you more visual (read), auditory (call), or kinesthetic (start plugging)?

We all process information to some extent through all three senses, but there is generally one of the ways that is predominant for each individual. Learning how to direct marketing material in a way that reaches all three types is our goal.

Reaching Out Through V-A-K Metaphors

The first column in Figure 4.1 makes a generic statement. The columns next to the first show alternative ways the same information could be conveyed to achieve better communication with each of the three V-A-K types.

The list of words and phrases in Figure 4.2 can be useful in preparing ad copy for use in different media sources. The trick is to be able to insert enough of all three kinds of key words into your media advertising!

Figure 4.3 is a detailed description of a property. It could appear just as it is written for a newspaper or magazine ad, but see if you could make it more interesting by using words that will attract the attention of all three V-A-K types.

FIGURE 4.1 / V-A-K Communication

GENERIC	VISUAL	AUDITORY	KINESTHETIC
I really like this house.	I can just see myself living here.	Sounds like this is the right place.	You know, this just feels like our house.
I understand what you said.	I see your point.	I hear what you are saying.	I'm in touch with what you're saying.
This job can be done quickly.	The job will be done in a flash.	Just a snap of the fingers, and it is done.	With a hop, skip, jump, the job is finished.
This settlement statement is correct.	I know beyond a shadow of a doubt that it is correct.	That statement is accurate word for word.	The information given here is as solid as a rock.
I am not sure about that.	That is pretty hazy to me.	That doesn't really ring a bell.	I am not sure I follow you.
This house has a brick fireplace with a raised hearth.	Picture your family gathered around this beautiful hearth.	Hear the snapping wood and the corn popping.	Feel the warmth radiate out in the room.

FIGURE 4.2 / V-A-K Words and Phrases

VISUAL	AUDITORY	KINESTHETIC
Beyond a shadow of doubt	Clear as a bell	Chip off old block
Describe	Discuss	Demonstrate
Get an eyeful	Entertain me	Get a handle on
Get a perspective	Give me your ear	Get a load of this
Gleam in the eye	Hardly a peep	Be in touch with
Hazy idea	Heard voices	Gut feeling
Imagine that	Hold your tongue	Draw a picture
In view of	Listen in	Heated argument
Looks like	Loud and clear	Illustrate
Like a photo	Power of speech	Tasty
Mental image	Manner of speaking	Hot seat
Mind's eye	Outspoken	Lay hands on
Map out	Pay attention to	Intuition
Paint a picture	Rings a bell	Point out
Pretty as a picture	Purrs like a kitten	Feels just right
Take a peek	Tuned in	Moment of panic

FIGURE 4.3

Just Listed

Three-bedroom, two-bath, one-level house on ¾ acre bordering 4,000 acre lake. Yard has orange and grapefruit trees, flowering shrubs, and perennial flower beds. Glassed-in porch extends across back of house with French doors opening onto a 25-foot swimming pool. Pool area is screened in and has deck area with room for picnic table & lounge chairs. Interior of house has gray carpet in LR, DR, & BRs, with hall, kitchen, and baths in white tile. Large kitchen includes refrigerator/freezer, double oven, microwave, double sink with garbage disposer, and pantry. Washer and dryer plus storage cabinets are included in adjacent laundry room. Master bath has separate shower and toilet areas plus Jacuzzi tub. Ceiling fans in every room of the house, including the 2+ car garage. Property is located 2 ½ miles from the center of small town and 40 miles from major city.

Look over what you have written. Underline the words that will appeal to the visually oriented in red, the auditory in blue, and the kinesthetic in green. Which color shows up the most? More than likely, this is the way *you* process information. The most challenging part of using V-A-K in marketing is to come up with words that relate to a processing mode that you seldom use yourself.

TYPES OF ADVERTISING MEDIA

Marketing that comes under the general category of "advertising" is generally that which is prepared by one individual and then delivered to a third party for distribution to the general public. You can control the date on which your ad will appear, and, by paying a little extra, you may be able to designate placement on the printed page, or the time of day the radio ad will be run. However, even with the most exciting and enticing ad for your new listing that you can imagine, you literally have no control over whether your intended receiver will actually see or hear your message.

Typical advertising media can be grouped into the categories of print, audio/visual, and the Internet. Print and audio/visual are discussed in this chapter. Use of the Internet is covered in Chapter 5—21st-Century Marketing.

PRINT ADVERTISING

Regardless of the type of publication, there are ways to make any ad more attractive. Hal Douthit, creator and publisher of Re/Ad, a computer ad writing program for real estate, provided a list of 12 things (see Figure 4.4) that constitute good advertising in an article he wrote for *The Real Estate Professional,* July/August 2003. Also, see *http://www.adwriter.com* for more information on software programs for successful ad writing that are offered by Adwriter, Inc.

The printed word is the joy of the "visual processor" and the most commonly used form of advertising for real estate properties. In fact, most sellers and many agents never think beyond placing multiple ads in the newspapers. There are, of course, many other venues for print advertising. Several of the print options are discussed below with a summary of pros and cons for each option.

Newspaper Advertising

Every major city has at least one major newspaper. However, there are often more locally oriented papers in the suburbs or geographic

FIGURE 4.4 / "The 12 Things a Good Ad Does"

1. Stops the reader from turning the pages.
2. Works like a good salesperson by telling potential customers what a product will do for them.
3. Builds on a concept or idea. A reader must instantly recognize the concept being communicated.
4. Sells a product's benefits rather than its features. People buy based on what the product will do for them—not what ingredients it has.
5. Promotes the name of the company while visually creating an image for the firm.
6. Speaks to a specific group.
7. Provides all the facts a reader needs without providing too many.
8. Conveys its message simply. It is believable and honest.
9. Is supported by good company management and good customer service.
10. Remembers who the customer is and what would make that customer buy.
11. Is news. Readers say advertising is as important to them as other content.
12. Sells answers to consumers' current needs. Advertising sells to people's wants, not just needs. People *need* transportation, they *want* a Mercedes. They *need* clothing, they *want* Polo. Bringing it all back to real estate, "They *need* shelter, but they *want* a New Victorian With Sweeping Views!"

Source: The Newspaper Association of America (NAA).

sections of the city. Advertising a four-bedroom Colonial that is ideally suited for the move-up market in the *Fairfax Journal* might be more cost effective than running the same ad in *The Washington Post*. People often look for advertising in a local paper if they are already living in that area and wish to remain there but in a larger or more deluxe home.

In a city with a strong ethnic population, there may be a special newspaper in that language. If an agent is concentrating on a particular niche market of a particular nationality, ads placed in that paper—correctly translated into the language—could be very beneficial. If at all possible, speak with someone within your own network of contacts who speaks that language. Many things can be misconstrued or lost in translation. The translator must have knowledge of both the language and the real estate business. If you have no such personal contact, talk to the advertising manager of the paper. The ad manager should be able to assist you or suggest someone to translate your ad for you. The cost for such advertising will vary. Because it is a smaller publication, the cost may be higher than for the big city newspaper but well worth it because it will go to such a direct target market. Note: Always be sure to also advertise in English language newspapers at the same time to avoid any possibility of a fair housing violation.

It is also important to remember that there are other print options available besides your local newspaper. Nationally distributed papers such as *The New York Times* and *The Wall Street Journal* should be considered for special properties. For example, you may have a listing for a property in a town where a company is transferring employees from one of the large Northern metro centers. Vacation homes or resort properties are other likely candidates for national exposure. Advertising a typical three-bedroom townhouse for sale in Greenville, Kentucky, in *The Wall Street Journal* would hardly make sense. But advertising a waterfront property complete with boat slip at Islamorada Key might!

Shopper's tabloids that are typically distributed free of charge in both large and small cities or towns are another option for print advertising. Tabloid advertising is usually less expensive than regular newspapers and is generally distributed in a specific area, making it a good choice for local listings.

There are advantages and disadvantages of advertising in newspapers.

Advantages:

- The seller expects this type of advertising and is pleased to see the ad in print.
- The ad will reach a large number of people at one time.
- Prospective purchasers usually look first to the real estate section of the newspaper when they are interested in buying property.
- Classified ads are relatively inexpensive, at least compared to magazine, radio, TV, or direct mailing.

Disadvantages:

- Large picture ads are more effective but can be costly, especially in large city newspapers.
- Newspapers have no "shelf life" because they are usually thrown out daily.
- Only a small percentage of the people receiving the paper have any interest in the property being advertised. For example: *The Washington Post* reaches over 2 million subscribers in the metro area, but how many of them want to buy a townhouse in suburban Fairfax County?

Magazine Advertising

Magazines advertising real property range from very expensive, ultra-slick magazines promoting luxury properties to the popular book-size, slick-cover magazines featuring homes for sale in a particular geographic area. Some variety of the free "homes for sale" periodical is published in almost every city and town throughout the country. People relocating to an area often find these magazines helpful in order to gain an overall impression of the real estate market in their new location. Local people also pick up these free magazines at any of the many distribution points. In a "hot" market where properties are selling very quickly, the properties advertised may have sold weeks before, but the ad may still produce a call to the agent or at least to the company. The much more elaborate magazines advertising luxury properties for sale are very expensive to advertise in and should only be used for special properties; i.e., large estates, historic properties, high-cost resort homes, etc. Again there are advantages and disadvantages.

Advantages:

- Individual ads will be less expensive if the agent contracts for a full or half page ad to be run multiple times. In some cases, a brokerage firm contracts for several pages and makes them available to the agents for a fee.
- There is usually ample space available to write a more appealing ad using the V-A-K theory and to include exterior and interior photos of the property.
- Magazines have a longer "shelf life" because people tend to leave them lying on the coffee table or desk.
- The seller may be impressed to see the home advertised in a magazine.

- The magazine can be easily mailed to out-of-town clients or prospects.

Disadvantages:

- Deadlines are set far enough in advance from the actual printing of the publication that the property may be sold by the time the issue hits the streets. This is not a complete loss considering that the ad still promotes the agent's name and may result in a call from prospective buyers.
- Upper-scale luxury magazines are very expensive, and sellers of higher priced properties may pressure their agent to advertise there.
- The free magazines are only available at specific distribution points and may not be readily available to a large segment of the population.

Relocation Periodicals

The major relocation companies all produce their own type of magazine or tabloid-style periodical featuring properties throughout their relocation market area. You would need to make arrangements with the relocation company for placement of your ad.

Advantages:

- Goes directly to a target market that has a definite interest in relocating to your area
- In some cases, no cost to the individual agent

Disadvantages:

- Only goes to members of the relocation company network
- No agent control of placement or timing of ad

Infomercial

The print infomercial is a hybrid of advertisement and press release. They are always identified with the word "Advertisement," which is usually located in the upper right hand corner, but they do look more like a news story and may be perceived as such by the reader. Because you pay for an infomercial just as you would for a regular ad, you will have some control over the date it will appear in the newspaper. But it is generally better to stick to more general topics of information that are not date-sensitive. The infomercial should not be too long—two or three columns wide by six to eight inches deep is a good size. The text must say something that is actually newsworthy and of potential interest to the public. At the end of the article, include a statement like this: "For more information on this topic, contact Rebecca Salesleader at 555-1234 or e-mail her at rsalesleader@aol.com." Print infomercial topics that would be likely to catch the reader's eye might include the following:

- Is Mold Really a Danger?
- Who Pays for a Buyer Agent?
- How to Stage Your Home for Selling
- Is a Home Inspection Really Worth It?

Press Release

There are still many people who believe that if they see it in print, it must be true! And if an agent is able to have something actually published in the newspaper—not as an ad and not as an "infomercial"—it goes a long way toward promoting an agent or a property. Some local papers run a regular series of articles about unique or historic properties on the market. Others might run a column featuring newcomers to a neighborhood or old-timers retiring and moving away. Whatever the case, a well-written article submitted to the local paper, preferably along with a picture, may result in good advertising that is free!

Advantages:

- Consumers see it as "news," not as an "ad" and therefore it is more credible.
- There is no cost, other than preparation of the article.
- People are more apt to comment on having read the article than they are to mention seeing an ad.

Disadvantages:

- The agent must possess the skills to properly prepare a press release or be willing to pay a public relations firm to prepare it.
- The agent has absolutely no control over when, or if, the article will be published.
- This is not a useful tool for anything that is time sensitive such as an announcement of an upcoming homebuyer seminar on Saturday.

Fax Flyer

Although the facsimile or fax machine is hardly what you would call a new way to advertise, some companies and individual agents have found it to be an effective way to communicate with many people at the same time and at very little cost. For example, an agent can send out a flyer advertising a new listing or an invitation to an open house to many offices within the market area or to hundreds of individual agents at the same time. A fax can even be sent to thousands of addresses over your computer online access. Be cautious, however, of Federal Communications Commission (FCC) rulings. Unsolicited advertising is prohibited. There must be either an existing established business relationship with the intended recipient or the recipient must have provided written consent to receive such advertisements. The penalties are severe—up to $1,500 per facsimile sent. See *www.fcc.gov* for more information.

Advantages:

- You can reach many people almost instantly.
- There is no cost beyond the phone bill.
- Ad material can be prepared cheaply on an office computer.

Disadvantages:

- You have no control over the receiving end (may be discarded).
- You may irritate receivers if overused.

Flyers

In general a single-sheet flyer promoting one particular property or sale can be used in many ways. It can be sent out over the fax machine as described above, included with other mailings, or hand-delivered. A flyer delivered door-to-door in a townhouse project advertising an open house the following Sunday would be an effective and inexpensive way to promote the open house. Costs would be minimal; the photocopying of 200 sheets would be less than $20. A student could be hired to make the delivery for $5 to $10 per hour (or you can deliver them yourself giving you an opportunity to meet other homeowners). Keep the following tips for flyer design in mind:

- Less is more—don't overdesign.
- White space balances out heavy text.
- Use an easy to read font, no script or italics. (Times New Roman, Arial, and Comic Sans are all good—nothing smaller than 12 point, preferably larger.)
- Do not mix too many different fonts, stick with two or three at most.
- Use bold sparingly and only for emphasis.
- Remember to include your personal motto.
- Use your company name and logo.
- Include complete contact information: phone, fax, e-mail.
- Include a photo: a picture of the listing is best, possibly a computer graphic and/or your own photo.

Additional Print Sources

There are a few other print sources, discussed below, that can be productive outlets for promoting your name and expertise, although these venues may not always be appropriate for advertising a particular property.

Theater playbill. Community theaters and local high schools are often desperate for advertisers. While a small ad featuring an individual agent will have a "shelf life" lasting for at least the duration of the show, occasionally the same playbill is used throughout the season. Playbill advertising also engenders goodwill in the community. These ads are generally very inexpensive ranging from $25 to $75, depending on size.

School or church bulletin. Newsletters or flyers promoting bowling teams, soccer teams, the ladies auxiliary, Boy Scouts and Girl Scouts, church bible school, and so forth, are all potential sources for self-promotion ads. Typically these are low-key advertisements showing support for the community activity along with a brief statement of "I'm here to serve your real estate needs. Feel free to call with any questions." Generally, you are offering to cover the expenses of preparing the newsletter, flyer, or bulletin in recognition of your sponsorship. Cost will depend on the size, layout, and number of pieces distributed.

Yellow pages. The familiar "Let your fingers do the walking" ad for including your business in your local yellow pages of the telephone directory can work for your own institutional ad (promoting yourself, not a particular property). These ads are fairly expensive, compared to regular newspaper advertising, but they do have a long shelf life. You might question how many people look in the yellow pages for a REALTOR®. Actually, it is done fairly often by people moving into a new area who have not had an agent referred to them (or do not like the one they were referred to!). Yellow page ads vary in cost depending on the local telephone service but can be as much as $1,200.

Sponsorships. Every organization needs financial aid! Ads in their programs are always welcome but consider actually becoming a sponsor, providing T-shirts and/or caps for one of the following groups:

After-school program	Learning English class
Animal shelter	Little league team
Basketball team	Neighborhood watch
Bowling league	Park and recreation
Charity bike race, or	activities
walk-a-thon	School band or orchestra
Community band or	School clubs or societies
orchestra	School newspaper
Community theater group	School yearbook
Football team	Scout troop
Golf charity outing	Soccer team
Graduation program	Softball team
International student	
program	

As a sponsor, you should also show your support by attending the events as much as possible, learning the names of the participants and their family members.

Multiple-Listing Service

Although it is not usually considered to be a type of advertising media, the multiple-listing service (MLS) that is offered in practically every part of the country is, in fact, a form of print advertising. Some MLS systems are owned and operated by the local association of REALTORS®. Others may be private companies with close affiliation with the local REALTOR® association. Regardless of the name of the MLS system used in your market area, the concept behind this service is to provide a common source for brokers to advertise their listings along with an offer of cooperation and compensation to any other broker who will bring a purchaser for the property. The information printed out from computer access to the local MLS is available to all agents and may be given to prospective clients and customers. The printout may vary from a short, highly cryptic piece using abbreviations, such as BR, MBR, DR, FPL, ESIK, etc., to one that includes digital images of the home, a directional map, and a listing of nearby amenities. The primary market for the MLS listing is other real estate agents, who will then bring the property to the attention of their clients or customers. In preparing the general information for an MLS entry, it is key to remember who you are targeting. Make use of the V-A-K theory in the section left open for "Remarks" and try some catchy headlines as shown below. (*Hint:* these headlines work well for newspaper advertising also!)

Sophisticated Renovation!   A Ten on Any Scale!

Bring Your Imagination!   Traditional Elegance!

(for a fixer-upper)   Prime Location!

Today's Living at Its Best!   House with a View!

Classic Colonial!   Walking Neighborhood!

Country Charmer!   Large Yard End-Unit!

Convenience Plus!	Penthouse!
Vintage Elegance!	Cozy Bungalow!
Contemporary Glamour!	Sensational Split-Level!
Sunny Condo!	Motivated Sellers!
Mountain Views!	First Open House!
Waterfront!	New on the Market!
Lake View!	

Eye-catchers. Other phrases that you could include in your MLS remarks that might encourage other agents to show your listing would be indications of special features, a bonus offered to the selling agent, a sense of urgency on the part of the seller, or impending changes. Before using any of the following examples, however, you *must* have permission from the seller, preferably in writing:

- Special this weekend only—riding lawn mower conveys with full-price offer!
- Fourth of July Special—Brand new Bar-B-Q grill giveaway drawing this weekend!
- $1,000 bonus to selling broker for contract acceptable to seller!
- Seller says—BRING ME AN OFFER!
- Base price goes up 10 percent next week. Act now!
- Weekend get-away for two provided for sale this weekend!

AUDIO/VISUAL ADVERTISING

Psychological studies say that people remember only about 20 percent of what they either hear or see. That percentage doubles when the message is both heard *and* seen. Unfortunately, in some cases we only have the ability to view the message, as in all of the print advertising media plus flyers, postcards, and even e-mail. In other cases, we are only able to hear the message as with the telephone or radio.

The Telephone—Outgoing Calls

Possibly the most misused audio medium for marketing is the telephone. As a result of extreme overuse of telemarketing, the Federal Trade Commission (FTC) established the national Do-Not-Call Registry to enable consumers to stop receiving telemarketing calls that came across state lines. Individuals tired of receiving unwanted and uninvited calls can now register their phone number at *http://www.donotcall.gov/register* or by calling (888) 382-1222. You must call from the phone number you wish to register, either your home phone or wireless number. Early in 2004, the Federal Communications Commission (FCC) extended the FTC Do-Not-Call Registry to include calls made *within* a state. The new FCC ruling supersedes any existing state do-not-call rules, some of which did exclude real estate practitioners from liability. As of October 1, 2003, agents are prohibited from making any prospecting calls either in or out of their state to persons on the Do-Not-Call list. The only exception is for calls made to someone with whom you have an existing business relationship, which is further defined as 18 months after a business transaction and up to three months after a consumer inquiry or application.

Neither the FTC nor the FCC rulings specifically prohibit cold calling; the rulings prohibit only calling those parties listed on the Do-Not-Call Registry. However, the necessity to purchase the list of names in the registry and to cross-check call lists against the registry every three months will obviously hamper the use of cold calling as a marketing tool. Businesses can receive the do-not-call list for up to five area codes for free, but a more extensive list may cost up to a maximum of $7,200. The penalty for violating the ruling is severe—up to $11,000 per call. A broker may not be found liable if it can be shown that the call was made in error; i.e., that the company maintains certain safeguards such as written procedures for compliance and updated lists of numbers. To avoid any chance of violation, many brokerage firms have established policies limiting prospecting calls made by their agents to those parties with whom the agents already have a business relationship, or those individuals who have requested a call for further information. For more detailed information on the Do-Not-Call Registry see *http://www.ftc.gov*, or *http://www.fcc.gov*.

The National Association of REALTORS® (NAR) has taken a position with regard to calling a FSBO (For Sale By Owner). NAR advises that as long as the agent is only calling to discuss a client's potential interest in the property and the agent is in no way soliciting the listing there is no violation. An argument is also made that by placing a For Sale By Owner sign in the yard, the seller is inviting calls made on behalf of an interested buyer.

The Telephone—Incoming Calls

Another side of marketing via the telephone totally within FTC or FCC limits occurs when a potential prospect makes the call to the real estate company. Unfortunately, in many offices the traditional "floor duty" or "agent on call" opportunity is treated casually and with little thought given to the potential for marketing of either the agent or a property. Remember, you never get a second chance at a first impression. The agent responding to the call has just a few minutes to effectively market his or her services. Agents should write out appropriate responses to the different queries that may come into the office and practice making these responses factual, interesting, and creative. The goal is to obtain the name and phone number and, hopefully, an appointment with the person on the other end of the line, not to merely answer questions. This is the right time to ask if the caller is already working with an agent. If not, the door is open to suggest that the caller come into the office to discuss how the agent could provide full representation in any future real estate transaction.

Radio

The biggest market for radio advertising today is the large number of commuters driving to work and those out shopping or running errands. Because there is no "mute" button on a car radio, listeners cannot tune out ads as they might do with television ads (of course radio listeners can switch to a different station). The confines of the car provide the advertiser with a captive audience. The trick for advertisers is to be sure that their ad is reaching the right audience for their product. It may not make much sense to advertise upper-scale, four-bedroom Colonials with a two-car garage on the favorite rock and roll station. If your target market is the 20-year-old to 30-year-old group interested in buying a first home, the "golden oldies" station is probably not the best choice either. Radio station sales executives have ample research data to help you determine who listens to which programs and when they are most likely to tune in. A little more money spent at the rush hour peak may be more cost effective than ten spots scattered throughout the normal workday hours. The number of spots contracted for does affect the total cost.

Advantages:

- The ability exists to reach a large audience at one time.
- The cost is relatively inexpensive, at least compared to TV. The cost also depends on the station and time slot selected for the ad.
- The ad can be updated fairly easily in order to remain timely.

Disadvantages:

- You must sign up for numerous spots in order for it to be cost effective.
- You have no control over who hears the ad.
- Listeners are often distracted and may have a limited attention span.
- Only a small percentage of the population is auditory. Psychological studies show that the majority of the population is visual or kinesthetic, with a smaller percentage of auditory processors.

Television

Because television provides an opportunity for the consumer to both see and hear the information, it is a natural venue for the promotion of products and services. Millions of dollars are poured into TV advertising every day, while millions more are paid to those who create and produce the ads. A 30-second slot on Super Bowl Sunday costs over 2 million dollars. A 30-second slot on prime-time TV can cost hundreds of thousands of dollars. Advertising on television does have the advantage of catching the attention of both visual and auditory individuals at the same time.

We remember twice as much if we both see it *and* hear it. Of course, that is assuming that we did not hit the mute button or head for the kitchen to grab a snack. Ever wonder why the ads are always louder than the show itself? They know what you are doing!

TV advertising for the average real estate company or practitioner is usually out of the question due to cost. The National Association of REALTORS® has run an effective series of ads appearing on network stations over the past several years promoting a positive image of the REALTOR®. Every REALTOR® member contributed a small additional amount to the annual dues to pay for the ads. Apparently, the ad campaign was successful. Follow-up surveys by NAR indicate that the general public seems to have a higher appreciation today of the value that the real estate professional brings to the real estate transaction than in the past. Large franchise companies such as ReMax, ERA, or Century 21 also run institutional ads, promoting the expertise of their franchise companies located all over the country. These ads provide TV exposure for small branch offices belonging to the franchise that would not be able to afford such advertising on their own. A large independent company might find it worthwhile to advertise on a local news slot or during local weather or sports event broadcasts. The cost of this advertising can then be spread out over several branch offices.

Cable Television

Almost every urban area in the country offers some type of cable TV real estate station. For a fairly nominal cost, agents can present a property that they have listed for sale or can promote their own expertise as a buyer's agent, second home expert, or other specialty. The cost varies depending on the geographic location and the number of times the ad is run, but a typical contract for multiple properties would cost approximately $30 to $60 per showing.

Because the real estate channel usually loops during a 24-hour day, the individual ad will appear many times throughout the day. Surprisingly, there is a fairly large audience for this type of programming. For example, people relocating to an area may automatically turn on the TV to search for such a station. Other real estate agents may tune in from time to time just to stay familiar with the market. Some real estate offices leave the TV turned on to the real estate channel in the waiting area of the office. And, of course, the sellers are thrilled to see their precious home featured so nicely on TV. For seller appreciation of what you do for them, this may actually be your biggest bang for the buck! The cost to run an ad on the real estate channel varies from city to city but will certainly be less than an ad in one of the luxury home magazines and most likely will even cost less than a picture ad in the Sunday open house section. Costs range from $30 per showing with $250 to $600 for a contract for a set number of days that the ad will run.

Advantages:

- The seller is impressed with the prestige of having picture ad on TV.
- It is relatively inexpensive.
- Easy to submit; cable TV sales reps pick up information at agent's office.
- Those who do watch are genuinely interested.

Disadvantages:

- Not many people actually watch the station.
- Advertiser must sign up for a series of runs to be cost effective.

- Cable TV rarely provides a buyer for the property, although the value for agent name recognition and seller satisfaction make it worthwhile.

Another way that cable TV may be a viable component of your marketing strategy would be for the broker to sponsor an infomercial that provides programming of interest to homeowners. A sales representative from the cable TV company that operates the real estate channel will be happy to provide you with information on how you can prepare your own infomercial. Companies that would be appropriate partners for a real estate company to sponsor would be home inspection companies, environmental testing services, settlement attorneys, mortgage companies, or moving and storage companies. Programs that might be of interest to viewers could include short programs on the following:

- The health hazards of radon, mold, or lead-based paint
- Special financing programs for police officers or teachers
- Local soil conditions problems such as marine clay or sinkholes
- Seasonal problems such as beetle infestation, mosquitoes, or locusts

The infomercial would, of course, include a prominent display at the close of the program with the name and phone number of the sponsoring company with an offer to provide additional information on the subject by just calling the real estate office. One listing to be run four times a day for seven days will cost about $350 in most markets.

Yard Signs and Riders

Just as the business card acts as an introduction of the agent, the yard sign is the introduction of the house to a prospective buyer. If the yard sign is dirty, crooked, ugly in color, or difficult to read, it can totally negate a lot of the other good marketing techniques that are being used for this property. The best-looking yard signs today are those generally provided by the brokerage company and installed on sturdy posts by a sign installation company. The brokerage firm may cover the cost of the sign or back-charge individual agents. Charges range from $30 to $80 to cover both installation and removal. Many people feel that the metal signs that agents just stick in the ground are out-dated today and give the impression that this property is not a particularly important listing for the agent.

Available with a multitude of different messages, small sign riders are often attached to the big company sign. Most important, of course, is the agent's name and phone number. Other riders like "must see inside," "swimming pool," "all-new kitchen," or "seller financing available" are intended to cause a casual observer to want to see more of the property. Following the advertising philosophy of getting your face in front of the public whenever possible, many agents today also include their picture on the yard sign.

An interesting combination of visual plus auditory is the talking yard sign. This is a sign that is placed on the property that will "talk" to the person who stops in front of it. Some are triggered automatically; others require the listener to push a button. Either way, more detailed or colorful information can be given about the property than is being seen from the outside. It may create an atmosphere of intrigue that will motivate the listener to call the listing agent for a special tour of the house. You can order a free video information packet from "Talking House" by calling (800) 211-6222 or faxing your business card to (888) 923-6222. More information on "talking houses" can be found at *www.talkinghouse.com,* *www.audiohousetour.com,* and *www.rrsta.com/radiosign.* The pros and cons of talking signs are as follows:

Advantages:

- Shows agent is interested in state-of-the-art tools
- Makes it possible to provide more information than on the brochure

Disadvantages:

- Signs are subject to vandalism
- Talking signs are much more expensive than ordinary yard signs

Other Signage

The signage for any individual property is hopefully only there for a matter of weeks—a few months at most. For the promotion of an individual agent, there are several other types of more permanent signage that may be an effective marketing tool.

Billboard. Billboards erected at the main highway entrances into a town have proved effective for some agents, especially in smaller towns or cities. The billboard usually has a picture of the agent plus something about that agent's special skill or ability. Billboard signs can be very costly at $30,000 to $40,000 a month and may require lighting and maintenance.

Moving van sign. A new marketing tool used in other industries as well as real estate is to have a sign on the back or side of a moving van, delivery truck, etc. The newest type is the sign that actually changes as the vehicle moves down the road. This attracts the attention of nearby drivers, especially if traffic is heavy and slow. Because this is a new product with limited availability, there are no average prices available yet.

Grocery cart. The local Safeway, Publix, or Food Lion may offer an opportunity for someone to advertise on the back of each grocery cart. The tool may not be too expensive, but it is also not located where most people normally look when seeking a real estate agent. Costs around $500 per month for a 10-inch by 10-inch ad on all carts in one store.

Bench. Depending on the community, there may be a marketing opportunity for signage on the back of a park bench or a waiting bench at a bus stop. There are also opportunities for ads as inserts both inside and outside a bus, trolley, or subway car. Signs on a bus or at a stop run about $2,000 per month in major market areas.

Signage and Name Recognition

An important aspect of advertising signage is the subliminal effect created. When prospective customers start to think about looking for a real estate agent, they may subconsciously pick the one whose name looks familiar. We know that the majority of leads come from one person recommending a particular agent to another person, but there are still many prospects who become interested in making a move and either don't ask anyone for a suggestion or do not know anyone else who has recently worked with an agent. The first-time homebuyer who has just moved into the community, recent immigrants to the city, or persons relocating to a new area will often call the agent whose name they remember seeing frequently.

Another facet of sign advertising is familiarity. An attractive well-placed sign in front of a property located on a busy street leading into a residential community will often make outsiders believe that the agent has many listings in that community. Seeing that same sign every day has left an impression that there are numerous such signs posted all over the area.

DIRECT MARKETING

Direct marketing does not rely on the hope that a prospective customer or client will pick up a newspaper or turn on the radio or TV. Direct marketing takes the concept of advertising one step further by leaving delivery of the message much more within the control of the marketer. Whether done by mail, phone, e-mail, or face-to-face the emphasis is on bringing the message to the person most likely to be interested in receiving it.

Direct Mail

The direct mail approach can vary from a handwritten note sent to one individual to a 300-piece mailing to a specific housing subdivision. The point is to use the mail as a means of reaching a specific target audience. The more specific the target, the higher the level of response that can be expected. For example, an agent seeking listings in a 300-unit condominium project could just send out a general mailing to every occupant of the project. A much more defined target would be to send a personalized letter to each absentee owner showing how market conditions have changed in the past few years and including information on comparable units that have sold recently. The key is to determine the target for the message and then choose the best way to reach that target.

Direct mail to individuals.

Preferably handwritten but if done by computer try to add a personal handwritten note across the bottom of the page; i.e., "How's Susie doing in her first year in college?" or "Did Tommy enjoy Boy Scout camp last summer?" or "Has your Siamese cat had another litter of kittens?" Use a hand-written address and first-class postage.

Target: Members of sphere-of-influence list
Message: I have a new career.
Benefit: I can help you with real estate questions.

Dear _____,

Just a quick note to let you know I have embarked on a new career in real estate. I passed the state exam last week and have affiliated with ABC Realty. If I can answer any questions that you may have about the real estate market in our area, just give me a call. I will always be happy to help you or any of your friends. Look forward to hearing from you—

Direct mail to absentee owners.

Computer-generated letter and envelopes from mailing list available through city tax records. Sign individually and send by first-class postage.

Target: 50 absentee owners in Highview Condominium
Message: I am marketing Highview Condominium.
Benefit: Information regarding increased prices

Dear Owner of Highview Condominium, (use correct owner name if available)

My name is _____ of ABC Realty. I have recently begun concentrating my marketing efforts on Highview Condominium. In doing my initial research, I noticed that you have not actually lived in your unit for several years. It occurred to me that you might not be aware of how much prices have escalated in our city over the past three years. Due to an unprecedented demand for housing within the city, the asking price for condominium units throughout the city has increased over 20 percent in the past year. A unit very similar to yours at Highview sold last month for _____.

If you would like more information about the current status of the market in the area, or specifically for Highview Condominium, feel free to either call me at (800) 111-1234, or e-mail me at _____.

Look forward to hearing from you,

Direct mail to single-family housing development.

Computer-generated letter and envelopes to mailing list derived from county tax records.

Target: 300 homes in Happy Acres subdivision
Message: I would like to list your home.
Benefit: A free consultation for "staging" your home

Dear Resident of Happy Acres, (use owner name if available)

Hello. My name is _____. I am with ABC Realty, and we are currently looking for prime quality single-family homes to add to our list of properties for sale in Lake County. We know that a home that is artfully and attractively presented will bring the best price possible. As a special incentive for you to list your home with us, we are offering to provide you with a free consultation with "Make It Pretty," a company that specializes in what is known as "staging" a home. The "Make it Pretty" consultant will give you suggestions for ways to de-clutter rooms, decide on color schemes, and many other ways to prepare your home to show at its best advantage. This $350 value will be given to every seller who lists with ABC Realty in the next three months. Call me today for more information on ways to make your home become the "prettiest on the block!" You can reach me at 000-1234 or by e-mail at

_____.

Postcards. Most bulk mailings end up in the trash before they are ever opened. Postcards at least have the benefit of being noticed while on the way to the circular file. A regular series of postcards sent into a home may help establish an agent's name as long as the postcards always have a consistent image; same picture, same lettering, same colors, etc. The message should vary, but the goal is to have instant name recognition just by the overall look of the card. You can create a postcard shell that includes your picture and contact information on one side, leaving the other side open for your message. Use bright colors, have your name in the largest font, and be sure to include your picture. Even if you do not think you are very photogenic, marketing experts always stress the importance of "keeping your face in front of the public." People are more comfortable with a familiar face—even if it's only been seen on a postcard. These cards can then be used for just listed, just sold, invitation to open house, invitation to homebuyer seminar, and other ideas. Once the shell is provided, the message will only have to be printed on one side. You can also take advantage of the cheaper postal rate for postcards rather than for a first-class mailing. Don't be afraid to be different. Some very successful agents include a picture of their family pet, their children, or something reflecting their favorite sport or hobby like skiing or gardening.

A variety of already prepared postcards are available from many commercial companies. These companies advertise on the Internet, in trade magazines like REALTOR® *Magazine* and *The Real Estate Professional*, and can be found at vendor booths at local, state, and national REALTOR® convention trade shows. One series features recipes; another has classic homes, such as the White House, Taj Mahal, Buckingham Palace, etc.; others portray famous gardens, historical landmarks, patriotic themes, dogs, cats, you name it! The cards can be ordered as a shell, or as a series of monthly mailings. It is unrealistic to expect great returns from using a direct mail piece on a "one-time" basis. Repetition is the key to success. A sampling of companies offering postcards as well as other marketing materials can be seen at *www.ReaMark.com, www.sellsmart.com, Adinfo@expresscopy.com, EVGcreations@aol.com, www.direct-color.com, www.NewHomeSale.com,* and *www.marketyour property.com.*

Just listed and just sold cards. The commercial companies that offer prepared postcards also have an interesting variety of the popular just listed or just sold cards. Large independent companies and franchises often have their own style of cards that are made available to their agents at a minimal cost. The important thing is to understand the purpose for the mailing. Is it to sell the property listed or is it to promote the listing agent?

For Example Jack T. has a new listing in Greenwood, a townhouse development of 150 very similar units. If he sends out 150 just listed cards into Greenwood, does he expect to find a buyer?

Probably not, unless the development has a number of rented units. Does he wish to become known in a new area? This mailing could be a start for his campaign. Advertising gurus tell us that it takes up to eight repetitions of a name before anyone ever remembers it. He will need to map out a continuing program of mailings before this goal will be reached. Does he want to impress his seller? This mailing may help but only as long as there are other strategies included in his marketing plan. The important issue is for Jack to understand why he is doing the mailing. Only then will he know whether it has any value.

Is the just sold card to provide useful information for the neighbors or is it to brag a little about the success of the agent? If Jack prefers to work as a buyer's agent and is not really interested in obtaining listings, sending out just sold cards when his townhouse listing sells is probably not worth the effort and cost. On the other hand, if he is interested in becoming a popular listing agent in that area, the just sold cards may have an impact on other homeowners who might be considering selling. Doing it to impress the owner of the townhouse would not make much sense. The seller is as impressed as he will ever be now that the house is sold. Unless this seller has other properties to sell, Jack's time and money could be better spent on seeking new prospects.

Newsletters. One old standby of the traditional geographic farming tool is a monthly newsletter sent to all residents within a designated farm community. A *farm* is a subdivision, or section of town, where the agent has chosen to become known as the "expert." The newsletter usually contains a list of homes recently listed and/or sold and something like household tips or tasty recipes. Studies have found that senior citizens still enjoy this type of mailing, but today's younger rising seniors—the baby boomers—are only interested in reading about issues that may be significant to them or their community. The current generation of homebuyers and sellers is not likely to appreciate any type of newsletter unless it comes over the Internet and contains up-to-the-minute information that is relevant to their particular needs.

Current sales prices are always interesting to a homeowner, but other topics that might make them read and remember the name of the sender would be information about a zoning change or school redistricting that could affect the neighborhood, a possible solution for a pest problem (like mosquitoes, fire ants, corn borers, etc.), or a new financing option that could make refinancing attractive. A special news bulletin, either sent by mail or e-mail, that is only sent when there is a topic of interest may be more effective than a regular issue sent monthly whether there is anything to say or not.

For Example A large townhouse project in Fairfax County, Virginia, was originally built with aluminum wiring. Over the years, the wiring tended to cause problems and, in some cases, even fires. The agent who farmed that development kept everyone well informed of the problem and of possible solutions including the projected cost of replacement and a list of providers. His newsletters were sent out regularly on a monthly basis, but he tried to always include some item of news that would be of interest to the homeowners. He also included all community activities for both adults and children and, in fact, sponsored some of the events, such as the Halloween pumpkin carving contest and Fourth of July parade. His newsletter was only one part of his overall marketing campaign for that neighborhood but was something that people looked forward to receiving each month.

PERSONAL PROMOTION

If there is one point on which all advertising/marketing executives would agree it is that there is no substitute for word-of-mouth or personal referrals. When a friend says "you ought to try this brand of shampoo," "come try out my new car," or "you must give my real estate agent a call," it is worth more than thousands of dollars in general advertising. Agents can market themselves in many ways through the various advertising media already discussed, but there is also a vast arena of personal promotion where the agent has complete control over what is prepared and how it is distributed.

Stationery and Business Cards

Thanks to fax machines and e-mail there seems to be little use for stationery today, but there are still occasions when written correspondence is appropriate. Nicely printed stationery on a good quality paper is a worthwhile investment for those occasions.

Your business card is your most important entry into marketing yourself. It is usually the first thing you give people and immediately establishes a first impression. A cheap card that was obviously thrown together on a home computer does not say much about the quality of workmanship or knowledge of the agent handing out the card. On the other hand, a card that looks too "slick" or contains too hard a sales pitch is about as well received as the dinnertime call from the telemarketer who keeps using your first name repeatedly.

A well-planned card printed on quality stock that says something about your particular area of expertise but that is not cluttered with too many initials or titles conveys a silent message that you are a true professional. And, don't forget about using the back side of the card. A calendar, list of emergency phone numbers, or a homebuying checklist will make your card stand out and encourage the potential customer or client to keep it. Business cards cost anywhere from $40 to $100 per thousand, depending on the quality of the paper.

To see or not to see. The question of whether or not to include your picture on the business card is open for debate. Marketing experts will tell you to get your face in front of the public every time you can—on your card, your signs, your stationery, your ads. Another school of thought thinks your picture on the card looks "tacky." Regardless of your personal reaction, there is a lot to be said about the longer shelf life of a card with a picture. Think back to last Christmas. You may have thrown out most of the cards, but did you keep the one that had a picture of your second cousin's new twins? And you probably hardly know your cousin! When Sunday open house lookers return home, they usually discard most of the cards they have picked up, but they will often keep the one with the picture. It's just a fact of advertising life—people tend to hang on to pictures. You have to make your own decision about how you want your card to best represent you.

Targeted Directories

Agents who have completed additional education courses may have earned a special designation. They now have the right to include on their card and other marketing materials the fact that they are now a CRS (Certified Residential Specialist), an ABR (Accredited Buyers Representative), or others such as CIPS (Certified International Property Specialist) or the At Home with Diversity designation granted by NAR. The importance of the designation may vary depending on the target audience. Agents certified in various fields are then listed in directories published by the different organizations. The directories are also available on the Internet. In some cases, professional credentials seem to make more of an impression on older consumers. Younger potential customers may be primarily interested in what you can do for them today. In any case, the ability to present a knowledgeable, professional appearance backed up by confidence and experience is essential.

Personal Brochure

A personal brochure is basically a business card carried several steps further. Large companies often provide a suggested format, and many commercial companies will set up a brochure for you based on your information. The cost varies tremendously depending on whether you outsource the project or attempt to prepare one using home computer software such as Microsoft Publisher. One problem with a printed brochure is that it can not be edited easily, so changes in your area of expertise, your target audience, or even your appearance may make the brochure become obsolete too rapidly. Remember, poorly done is worse than not done at all.

Personal brochure tips. Things to include in a personal brochure include the following:

- Two-paragraph biography. Focus on professional skills, educational background, accomplishments, and community ties.
- Professional photo. No glamour shots, excessive jewelry, or suggestive poses. Dress appropriately for the image that you wish to convey.
- Your personal marketing motto or slogan.

- List of the communities you serve.
- Professional affiliations and memberships.
- Complete contact information by address, phone, fax, and e-mail.
- Your company logo and brief information about the company.

Brag Book

Similar in content to a personal brochure but usually much larger is an agent "brag book." Generally presented in a standard picture album, the brag book has information about the agent's credentials and successes. There may be pictures of properties that the agent has either listed or sold over the years; sometimes including pictures of the happy homeowners with their smiling agent. Letters of praise from satisfied clients are a very good item to include. For an agent who successfully works in a given area, a schematic plat of the subdivision showing all of the properties where the agent has either listed, sold, or rented a home is very impressive.

To actually sit with a prospective client and go through the brag book page by page would be tedious for the agent and boring for the prospect. The best idea is to leave the book overnight or for a few days for prospects to look over at their leisure. That is also a good excuse for a return visit to pick up the book.

Toys and Gadgets

Millions of dollars are spent each year on the various toys, household gadgets, calendars, pens, etc., etc., etc., that are given away by real estate agents. Their purpose is (1) to attract the attention of the prospect, and (2) to reinforce the name of the agent.

Remember, though, repetition is the name of the game. Several hundred dollars spent on a one-time marketing push is not likely to yield much in the way of results. All too often, an agent will spend dollars for some type of giveaway and take time to actually go knock on doors in a neighborhood, and then wonder why nothing ever resulted from all this time and money. If it takes multiple times before a name is even recognized, a one time visit with a gift of a rubber jar opener is not likely to result in a bona fide client. You must know your target market, prepare a total marketing plan, and then select an appropriate giveaway that fits into this plan. Visit trade shows at conventions and read the ads in professional magazines for companies offering marketing tools for giveaways. A few marketing tool vendors are Fine Incentives at (800) 752-FINE, *www.realestatefarmaids.com, www.flagco.com,* and *www.scgifts.biz.*

Personal Promotion of Properties

The personal promotion of properties boils down to (1) the open house and (2) the broker open, both discussed below.

Open house. In addition to all of the advertising methods discussed earlier, there are also many good opportunities to personally promote the properties that you have listed. Despite some agents' opinions to the contrary, the open house remains a viable tool in the marketing arsenal for most agents. Holding a property open for a few hours on Saturday or Sunday, or even on a weekday evening, gives the listing agent an opportunity to gauge the reaction of prospective buyers to the appearance and amenities of the property. It also provides an opportunity for agents to expand their list of prospects for this, as well as other, similar properties in the same area or price range.

Making it count double. Personal promotion of your listings also provides an opportunity for personal promotion of yourself. Come prepared for your open house with information about other new listings—attractive, eye-catching information, not just a copy of the MLS printout—and you will double the value of your efforts. Be prepared to talk about other listings that are similar to the property being shown or that are in the same general area or price range.

Whether the purpose for the open house is to try to sell the property or to promote the services of the agent, the key is to make it something distinctive. Plan some special feature that will make prospective lookers remember that particular house. It could be some sort of simple refreshments, coordinated perhaps with a particular season or holiday, such as cider and pumpkin bread for Halloween or punch and fruitcake cookies for Christmas. For a home with playground equipment or a tree house in the yard, invite the children who tag along with their parents to the open house to stay outside and play. Bring along a responsible person to supervise the outdoor activities. A house with a pool offers an ideal place to serve lemonade and cookies while discussing the other features of the house. Or plan to pop corn or roast marshmallows in the raised hearth fireplace in the family room. Anything that makes this particular house memorable when today's Sunday open house attendees return home is a successful marketing technique.

Special promotion features for the house also provide more attention to the listing agent. Prospective sellers often visit local open houses to "shop" for a listing agent. Make yourself and your style of marketing memorable to all visitors.

Broker's open. A variation of the public open house is a broker's open where agents and brokers from other companies in the same area are invited to see the property. A broker's open is usually held during the week around lunchtime, after the typical weekly morning sales meeting. In fact, broker opens are sometimes referred to as "feed the REALTOR® day," with refreshments ranging from stale donuts to a full lunch of shish-ka-bobs and ice cream sundaes!

The purpose for a broker's open is to provide an opportunity for the listing agent to point out any special features of the home to other agents. This is a particularly effective tool for a property that might otherwise be overlooked; i.e., an exceptionally well-updated home in an area of older properties or a property that is located off the beaten track that might seem to be too much trouble to locate in order to show it. Holding a broker's open for one townhouse situated in the midst of 100 other similar properties that is easily accessed from a main road and that has nothing special to offer in the way of financing or amenities is most likely a waste of your marketing budget and time.

IN CONCLUSION

Good marketing is a matter of quality, not quantity. You want to spend your time, energy, and dollars where you can anticipate the most return. Write ads in a V-A-K way that will attract the attention of all types of consumers. Use a mix of media: print, audio/visual, TV, and the Internet. Concentrate on direct marketing techniques where you can expect more direct response. Select marketing tools designed to reach out to your chosen target market. Whenever possible, take the opportunity to market yourself along with your listed properties. Be sure to track which of your marketing efforts brought the most results. And remember that marketing is a matter of long-term planning and action.

5

21st-Century Marketing

For many years, the real estate professional stood at the gateway to information about properties that were for sale. Only REALTORS® or other state licensed salespersons or brokers had access to information the public wanted—what homes are for sale, how much are they, how many bedrooms, is there a fireplace, what else is included in the asking price, and, ultimately, how can I make an offer to buy this property? The key to the gate was the multiple-listing service (MLS). Through the MLS, brokers throughout the country agreed to share the information about their listings and to make an offer of cooperation with other brokers in the area who might have a buyer for one of their listings.

A CHANGING FOCUS

Today's buyers are able to find everything they want to know about houses for sale all on their own on the World Wide Web. *Realtor.com, Homeseeker.com, Cyberhomes.com,* and other housing information sites offer pictures, a full description of the house, and even a map with directions on how to get there.

Where does that leave the old "gate keeper"? The service the real estate agent of the 21st century has to offer is the knowledge of how to put a deal together and get it to closing successfully. Further education, such as sales training and state-required continuing education, gives the real estate "pro" the ability to guide the client through the myriad of detail and paperwork involved in any real estate transaction. Life experiences provide the "pro" with the wisdom to anticipate and resolve problems that may occur. As the CEO of a large real estate firm once said, "I've never seen a computer yet that can resolve the problem of a leaky basement!"

Is a Web Presence Worth It Financially?

In a random telephone survey of 1,000 residential and commercial REALTORS®, the NAR Research Division found that real estate practitioners with a Web site earned about twice as much as those who do not have one; i.e., the average income for those with a Web site was $90,000 with $10,000 in total expenses, and the average income for those without a Web site was $45,500 with $6,000 in total expenses. (Quoted in *REALTOR*® *Magazine,* June, 2002.) The importance of a Web site is further demonstrated by the statistics gathered by the NAR in its 2003 publications (see Figure 5.1).

FIGURE 5.1 / Real Estate and the Web in 2003

68% of REALTORS® had a Web page

86% of REALTORS® used e-mail in their real estate practice

57% of REALTORS® generate at least some of their business online

65% of homebuyers used the Internet as an information source

72% of Internet homebuyers drove by or viewed a home they saw online

20% of FSBOs used the Internet to help sell their home

18% of Internet homebuyers found their agent online

Sources: 2003 REALTOR® Magazine Media Information Kit and The 2003 National Association of REALTORS® Profile of Home Buyers and Sellers.

There are several possible Web sites, discussed below, that you can use for marketing yourself and your listed properties.

Your company Web site: Make sure your current agent profile, your e-mail address, and your telephone extension or direct line are on your agent page within your brokerage site. (While cost varies by company, it is occasionally free.)

Realtor.com: You can purchase your own Web page on this national Web site for real estate listings and real estate sales agents. Clients shopping for a real estate sales agent in your market can learn more about you on this site. (The cost is approximately $600 per year.)

Your own Web site: A must-have for all agents. Once it is set up, it can move with you if you change your broker affiliation. Develop content for your personal Web site to provide information and resources for potential clients. Be sure to have your Web site seeded in the top search engines and enjoy 24/7 advertising for your real estate sales business. (The cost is approximately $100 per year if self-maintained and $500 to $1,000 a year if you hire it done, depending on the number of pages you build.)

WEB SITE DESIGN

Because most Web site developers are technology oriented and do not have the visual skills of a graphic designer, the design for your site should be created by a graphic designer. Online brochures that are not interesting will not attract potential clients to you, so plan your site carefully. After visiting other agents' Web sites to get a feel for what the public is viewing on other sites, make yours better! Be sure you are comfortable with whatever your Web master or Web designer comes up with. The most clever idea in the world means nothing if it does not portray the professional image that you have determined is you. Important skills to look for in selecting a graphic designer include the following:

- Breadth and depth of work as shown in portfolio
- Original concepts and ideas
- Ability to represent concepts, designs, and related rationale
- Several years of successful experience
- Types of products or companies represented

When designing your Web site, keep in mind the following three things about typical Internet consumers:

1. They like the anonymity that protects them from unwanted interaction.
2. They like to be in control of communication and keep it impersonal.
3. They appreciate that it gives them information making them more educated so that they feel they can shop more efficiently.

What Not to Do

Jack Nielsen, an Internet usability expert whose company is focused on Web site content and navigation, provides the following list of top ten mistakes in Web design:

1. Use of frames. (Usually requires extra scrolling that clients may not do and is also more difficult to print out.)
2. Gratuitous use of bleeding edge technology. (Don't get too fancy just because you can!)
3. Scrolling text, marquees, and constantly running animations. (They may catch *too* much of the viewer's attention.)
4. Complex URLs. (Your URL is your universal resource locator, in other words, your World Wide Web address; keep it simple and easy to find.)
5. Orphan pages. (Don't leave a page isolated or with no contact information.)
6. Long scrolling pages. (The viewer clicks "delete" because there is too much information.)
7. Lack of navigation support. (When you can't get there from here!)
8. Nonstandard link colors. (Stick with blue because everyone's used to it.)
9. Outdated information. (This is the kiss of death in what is supposed to be up-to-the-minute technology.)
10. Overly long download times. (Another excuse to hit the delete button; viewer thinks information is never coming up.)

What to Do

This is your Web site so make it truly yours. Remember, the average viewer attention span is not very long—somewhat like "surfing" on the TV—and you need to keep Web surfers interested. Provide links to other Web sites that may be of interest to them instead of cluttering up your own page with too much data. And be sure to include your name and contact information on every page. Finally, try to include as many of the following content suggestions as you can without getting too lengthy:

- About you: Your real estate professional profile
- Contact information for you: e-mail address and link, phone numbers, fax numbers, and your brokerage name and address
- List of areas or communities you serve
- Testimonials from clients, active or sold
- Properties for sale
- Weather information including monthly high and low temperatures for your area
- School information in your market
- How to sign up for your mailing list
- Links to home-finding and other home-related sites
- Process involved in selling a home in your market
- Process for purchasing a home in your market
- Relocation information for your market
- Map quest link so viewers can visualize the geography of your market area
- Your current listings (sometimes include sold listings)
- Specific niche information if you are marketing to a particular group
- How to request your newsletter, online or snail mail

- Site map
- Community information: licensing, taxes, voter registration sites
- Local sports, activities, cultural, tourist, etc., information

Domain names. Domain names vary in cost depending on the provider you choose, but generally domain names range from $35 a year for a basic one-page to five-page Web site to $100 per year for a 6-page to 25-page site. Also be sure to purchase an e-mail box for your Web site so visitors can e-mail you with questions. Two e-mail boxes run about $35 per year and must be attached to your domain name. (One e-mail box could be dedicated to local users and the other for relocation buyers.) Many agents today use their own name; i.e., *www.marknashrealtor.com;* a type of property, *www.beachfront.com;* or geographic area, *www.hamptons.com.*

Search engines. Now that you have a Web site, how will the surfers find you? You will need to have your Web site "seeded" (placed) into the top 10 to 20 search engines. "Seeding" refers to the "keywords" that individuals surfing the Web use to locate information.

> **For Example** Keywords for real estate might be *homes, house, condos, for sale, buyers, sellers, apartments, buyer's agent, broker.* It is also good to include key words for the city, county, or specific area that you serve along with the words *real estate.*

Having your Web site seeded within the top search engines is *not* optional. It is critical to success. Search engines "read" your site looking for the key words, so be sure to include target terms in the headline, subheadings, and, if possible, in the first line of each paragraph. Search engines search or "crawl" for "meta tags" embedded within Web sites. A *meta tag* is a descriptive string of words that help identify a Web site's content. In real estate, these meta tags might include: realty, real estate, townhouses, Florida, Tampa, relocation, top producer, foreclosures, and other related words. The differences between search engines rest in how they "crawl" the Web and acquire Web site information, as well as how they rank the information within their own site. Registering on a search engine is relatively easy, and there is usually no fee charged. The search engine page will show a link to adding a new site, then ask you for a few keywords or a brief description on the site. There are companies that will make your entries into the search engines for you. The cost depends on how many entries you choose, and how often you want your site registered. For example: The firm named 1st Page Submit charges $24.99 for entry into 10 engines every 14 days. By the way, if you are interested in having a high site ranking in a search engine, you should hire a search engine optimization specialist.

Search engines come and go, but generally a list of the 18 top-rated ones will include the following:

http://www.altavista.com   *http://www.aol.com/netfied*

http://www.directhit.com   *http://www.dmoz.org*

http://www.excite.com   *http://www.go.com*

http://www.google.com   *http://www.goto.com*

http://www.hotbot.com   *http://www.info.seek.com*

http://www.lycos.com   *http://www.magellan.com*

http://www.home.netscape.com   *http://www.snap.com*

http://www.msn.com   *http://www.webcrawler.com*

http://www.yahoo.com   *http://www.fastsearch.com*

You should also be aware of the "meta-search" engines that search through the top search engines and compile information for you. *Note:* You do *not* actually register your site on the "meta-search" engines such as *www.metacrawler.com, www.dogpile.com,* and *www.debriefing.com.* These meta-search sites derive their data from other sites such as Yahoo or Google.

Tips for creating effective Web sites. Increase your online real estate business by paying attention to the following tips:

- Include professional photographs, and keep them small. Don't overpower your page.
- Buy a Web site package that is expandable later to include extra pages and features.
- Know your Internet audience: determine your target market and focus your direction.
- Provide valuable consumer content. Have local information on parks, schools, after-school programs, little league, Girl Scout and Boy Scout programs; a column of frequently asked questions about buying and selling a home; a graphic design illustrating the homebuying process from contract to closing.
- Partner with transaction service providers. Mortgage brokers, attorneys, and home inspectors are some of the professionals who can contribute their expertise to your Web site.
- Make your site easy to navigate. Animated graphics, sounds, and pop-ups are neat, but they won't substitute for easy navigation for the consumer to get to the desired information.
- Return Web site requests in a timely manner. When real estate consumers start to e-mail you with requests to see homes or for more information, they are certainly a live

lead or prospect—respond within eight hours of receiving their e-mail.

■ Advertise your Web site address. Pay to have your site seeded in multiple search engines. List your Web site address on all of your advertising and on stationery and business cards, yard signs, anywhere your name appears.

■ Be different. With all the many real estate Web sites out there today, you have to be able to communicate your unique selling points to the Web consumer. Do you specialize in high-rise condos or suburban subdivisions? Are you expert in waterfront property or historic homes? Do you donate a portion of your compensation to your client's charity of choice? Look for ways to make your Web site stand out.

Links to other Web sites. Some people are reluctant to direct viewers away from their Web site by a link to another site for fear that they will "lose" the potential customer. Your Web site should open all link pages in a new window, so that your site visitor can close the link window and continue to navigate your site when they are finished with the link. Of course that risk exists because one link will often lead to another, and another, etc. Despite that inherent risk, links are still an excellent way to provide additional information for the viewer without making your personal Web site cumbersome. With a variety of links to outside sources, you make it possible for your viewers to quickly move to a page that may be of interest to them. It also increases the value of your site in their minds because you were able to provide them with answers to their questions and/or additional information on a particular subject.

For Example A link to the local school board would be of great interest to families with young children. A link to the parks and recreation page may be attractive to outdoor enthusiasts. A link to an article on home inspections could provide useful information for first-time homebuyers. A link to a local mortgage lender would be of great interest to potential purchasers.

Virtual tours. How many prospective buyers would like to be able to see the inside of a house for sale without actually having to make an appointment to visit the property with an agent? Thanks to digital photography and the Internet, virtual viewing is now possible. Some may still argue that this ruins the opportunity for you to show it to them yourself. But, on the other hand, until you have piqued their interest in the property in the first place, you may never have that opportunity. Although preparation of virtual tours can be very expensive if you outsource the whole process, you can prepare them yourself if you have a little expertise in using a camera and a computer.

And virtual tours do not need to be confined to showing houses. Try making a virtual tour of the community, showing schools, parks, shopping areas, and points of interest. For families with children, a separate tour of local schools featuring classrooms, sports facilities, laboratories, music rooms, library, and a few shots of students and faculty would be fun to make and of great interest to the prospective purchaser. See *www.eggsolution.com, www.virtual tours.realtown.com,* and *www.FTPHomes.com* for more information on setting up virtual tours of your listings that you can link to on your Web site. Call virtual tour photographers listed in your local phone book or call your local REALTOR® Association for referrals. If you would like to create your own virtual tour, you need a decent computer and the software application to turn your digital photos into a virtual tour. Supra, maker of the electronic keybox used by many local REALTOR® associations, has come out with a SUPRAeKEY that will not only let you enter the property but will let you view that property's listing plus listings of other properties, take pictures of the house while you are there, and exchange that information with other computers!

Real estate directories. Another avenue to pursue is the real estate directories. The oldest of these is the International Real Estate Digest (IRED) at *www.ired.com*. Other well-known directories are Realty Times (*www.realtytimes.com*) and the Real Estate Library (*www.relibrary.com*). These sites include useful information about buying and selling a home, various mortgage products, preparing a house for showing, and other topics of interest to consumers. Many of these articles are also very educational for real estate agents. Listings on most of these sites are free. Be sure to check with your local and/or state REALTOR® association. Many associations offer a free personal Web page to agents who are members of their association along with a general directory of agents listed by locality.

E-MAIL MARKETING

E-mail marketing is a good way for you to communicate with potential and active customers. Notices of free seminars, public open houses, and new listings can be sent to a large number of contacts with one click on the send button.

Tips for Using E-Mail

Following are some useful tips for using e-mail to market your-self and your listings:

- Use the subject line to state the purpose of your message. Keep it brief, five words or less. Longer subjects may not appear in some e-mail recipients' browsers.
- Add a complete and thorough signature. Be sure to include all of your contact information: address, telephone, fax, e-mail, and Web site. This can be set up to automatically appear at the end of every e-mail you send.
- Include a hot link in your e-mail so recipients can click directly to your (or your company) Web site.
- Pick up e-mail twice a day at the minimum, weekends included. You will receive e-mail seven days a week once you have a Web site. Be proactive and check to see what new cus-tomers are in your inbox. One of the joys of e-mail is that it eliminates the problem of crossing time zones.
- Do not send unsolicited e-mails. Ask permission before add-ing clients or prospects to your e-mail lists. Ask if they would like to be included on your newsletter mailing list—a perfect excuse to receive their e-mail address.
- Use auto-responders to acknowledge incoming e-mail mes-sages if you are out of town or tied up in a long meeting, clos-ing, or seminar. Your Internet service provider for e-mail can help you set this up. In your e-mail system under "options" look for auto-reply. Auto-reply, when activated, will automati-cally send a message to the sender of any message you receive. The most common use is to notify people when you are on vacation. You will be directed to a text box to write, submit, and activate your auto-reply option.

- Keep messages brief, concise, and to the point. Look for the "spell check" on your e-mail system and use it on every business-related message you send. It is well worth the time to catch typos and spelling errors.
- Stick to professional writing styles until you have established a more informal relationship with the receiving party.

The E-Mail Newsletter

A regular, snail-mail, monthly newsletter has been a marketing tool used by agents farming a certain geographic area for many years. The 21st-century approach to this is an e-mail newsletter. Elyse Harney, of Elyse Harney Real Estate in Salisbury, Connecticut, was featured in the *realtor.org* magazine where she shared her ideas for her "Country Journal." Her e-mailed newsletter informs people of upcoming community events and is sent out midweek to give people time to make weekend plans. She encourages people to visit her town by holding a contest to "name that historic site." A picture of the place is featured in the newsletter and the first reader to name it wins a weekend at a local bed and breakfast. Her Web site was named "Best Web Page" by the Connecticut Association of REALTORS® in 1999 and must be working—Ms. Harney netted more than $38 million in sales in 2001! (Source: *realtor.org/realtormag*, April, 2002.)

Where to send. You can rent a list of names from a reputable company that includes names of those who have indicated that they want to receive e-mail advertisements. But be wary of offers to provide you with lists of names categorized by geographic area, income, or house value. Lists that are sold featuring basic demographic information are inexpensive, but they are sold many times over to a variety of service and product vendors. You should look for name lists that drill much deeper. For example, length of time in the home would be a valuable piece of information for an agent or broker. If the individuals have been in the home for five years or so, they may be ready to move. According to NAR, the average homeowner moves every six years. Those recently divorced, the widowed, or new parents are also valuable prospects for the real estate professional because these types of life events lend themselves to changes in housing. Remember, antispam legislation makes it clear that you must only use e-mail to contact those persons with whom you already have a business relationship or who have requested information from you.

Can the Spam!

E-mail marketing has grown so much over time that the amount of unsolicited spam received today has literally turned many people against the whole idea. More and more consumers are resorting to antispam programs that do not allow any messages to come through unless the sender is already on the receiver's address list. This reinforces the importance of establishing a relationship with potential customers by requesting their e-mail address to add to your e-mail list.

The "Controlling Assault of Nonsolicited Pornography and Marketing Act," also known as the CAN-SPAM Act of 2003, created a single national standard designed to control the growing problem of deceptive or fraudulent commercial e-mail. The act does not ban commercial e-mails but does outline a series of practices that must be followed. The act exempts only "transactional or relationship messages" from complying with these practices. Communications between broker/agent and customer/client are probably covered, but messages attempting to solicit sellers or buyers who are not presently your customers or clients, are probably not covered. It pays to be safe, rather than sorry, because the fines will be steep.

OTHER WEB MARKETING CHOICES

Other Web marketing choices that you can discuss with your Web site manager are described below.

Listserv® is an electronic mailing list where Web site visitors can sign up to receive information on price ranges in a market, school reports, and other statistics they may find useful. Listserv® is the most common form of a mail list. "Listserv" is a registered trademark of L-Soft International, Inc.

Maillist is an automated system that allows people to send e-mail to one address, whereupon their message is copied and forwarded to all of the other subscribers to the mail list. People who have different kinds of e-mail access can participate in discussions together. For general reference, the following is a brief list of Internet terminology:

- blogs—An online journal where the person who keeps the blog is a "blogger." Postings on a blog are usually arranged in chronological order with the recent additions featured first.
- online newsletters—described above.
- reciprocal links—links to other Web sites of possible interest to the consumer.
- auto-responders—these keep the responder to your message from getting impatient.
- affiliate programs—partner with mortgage lender, moving company, etc.
- online yellow pages—enter yourself in local market area.

ONE FINAL TIP

And one last tip—use your Internet connection to further your own education. There is a wealth of information available literally right at your fingertips on just about any topic concerning real estate, marketing, legislation, education, and hundreds of others. Check out *Realty Times, Inman News, Broker Agent News,* and *Dean Jackson Newsletter.* The more informed you are, the more value you bring to the real estate transaction. The more value your client sees in working with you, the more referrals will come your way. The more referrals that come to you result in more successful business.

IN CONCLUSION

The 21st century brings a change in focus for the role of the real estate professional from that of the "gatekeeper" of information to that of a counselor who brings knowledge and experience to assist both buyers and sellers in the buying and selling of real estate. Important tools of 21st-century marketing are the Internet and e-mail. Use of the Internet should always be part of your daily work activity. Use your Web site to market yourself and your listed properties. Rely on e-mail to stay in constant contact with your clients. Build your own base of knowledge and stay up-to-date on current issues through Internet research. A well-informed agent brings value to the transaction—and value is what brings repeat and referral business to the agent.

6

Implementing
the Marketing Plan

In this chapter we will integrate all of the ideas discussed and outlined in the previous chapters into a marketing plan for a fictitious sales associate whom we'll call Rebecca Salesleader. We will illustrate each step of Rebecca's projected marketing plan and her subsequent actions.

ABOUT REBECCA

It's important to take a step back, every now and then, and ponder all the different life experiences we personally bring to the real estate marketplace. To help you begin thinking about this self-inventory, we will start by offering some background information on our fictitious sales agent, Rebecca Salesleader.

Rebecca Salesleader is an experienced agent who has been in residential real estate sales with ABC Real Estate in suburban

Chicagoville for five years. She has a four-year degree in interior design. With over $6 million in sales for the previous year, her gross income was $100,000. She has no professional designations, but she did upgrade her salesperson's license to a broker's license in her third year in real estate. She works an average of 60 hours per week. She has no personal assistant and splits her time administratively between her home and brokerage office. Rebecca is a breast cancer survivor, a board member for a non-profit regional theater company, and she donates time to the local chapter of Habitat for Humanity.

Rebecca's sales volume seems to have reached a plateau in the last year. While she wants to at least maintain her volume this year because she feels referral business will be soft in the next two years, she would really like to increase it by 15 percent. Her budget for marketing in the plan for year 200Y is 10 percent of her gross income or $10,000. This amount was chosen because most consumer product companies spend 10 percent of their gross revenue on product or service marketing.

REBECCA'S MARKETING AUDIT OF YEAR 200X

Rebecca's first step is to generate a marketing audit of her business from the previous year. From that audit she will learn what worked well and which marketing dollars and time were not well spent.

Rebecca will need to list all of her marketing activities as well as their costs. She will include public open houses and office telephone floor duty because they also represent marketing opportunities for her. Take a look at Rebecca's audit results for 200X.

Rebecca's Year

YEAR 200X	COST	RESULTS
Print Advertising		
Advertised 12 listings	$2,400	2 listings sold from ad (not as dual agent)
		1 closed buyer
Internet Advertising		
Set up one-page Web site	100	None
Purchased domain name	100	None
Telemarketing*		
Called 500 people from cross directory	25	One potential buyer
Floor duty 1 × 12 months	0	One closed seller
Direct Mail		
Sent 800 just listed/sold cards for 12 listings	612	One closed seller
Sent holiday cards to clients and farm list	100	One closed buyer referral
Public Open Houses		
24 classified ads	1,200	Two closed buyers
Radio		
Ten 30-second ads/morning drive time	1,800	None
Sponsorship		
One walk-a-thon team	350	One closed buyer
Total:	$6,607	5 Buyers and 2 Sellers
Gross Income:		$100,000

*This was previous year—before Do-Not-Call Registry existed.

Rebecca's Feedback from Marketing Audit

Print advertising. Because sellers expect their properties to be advertised, Rebecca must absorb this expense to be competitive in the marketplace. She did close one sale from a buyer who called on one of her listing ads, but her ads need to be updated and include cross-merchandising promoting herself in addition to the properties listed for sale.

Internet advertising. Rebecca is disappointed with the lack of response to her one-page Web site whose domain name is *north-suburbs.com*. She originally chose this name because she thought it would bring her wider market exposure. Because this did not work, she will need to consider a more personalized domain name.

Telemarketing. The cross directory, which each agent in her office helps pay for, will no longer be a useful tool next year as her office can't afford to purchase the do-not-call list. Rebecca feels that telemarketing for real estate agents is coming to an end anyway. This low-cost, fill-in-some-free-time cold-call marketing tool is obsolete. Meanwhile, the floor duty time for answering incoming calls to the office that Rebecca has been doing once a month for three hours has resulted in only one closed transaction. She wants to take a seminar to improve her skills at working with the public on floor calls. Rebecca realizes that she needs to replace telemarketing as a marketing tool. Many companies have this problem on a much larger scale.

Direct mail. Rebecca feels that her just listed/sold postcards look like everyone else's in the market. She believes that either projecting a new look or presenting something of benefit to householders needs to be implemented for her to invest in them again. The one closed seller that resulted from her just listed/sold cards was a result of a mailing sent out on a property that was on the market a very short time.

Open houses. Rebecca's public open houses netted her two closed buyers. With the large number of new agents coming into real estate, she feels that the available business is getting spread across a larger pool of agents. She was discouraged that the majority of buyers came to her open houses with agents or had already established agency relationships. From a time management perspective, she questions how productive all the time spent holding public open houses is for her business.

Radio advertising. Rebecca signed a contract for ten 30-second radio ads in order to help out a friend who was hired to sell radio ad time on a full commission basis. She felt like a local celebrity when friends and family talked about her ads. She had name recognition but no closed clients to show for her expenditure.

Sponsorship. After surviving breast cancer herself, Rebecca joined the local cancer awareness chapter and sponsored some friends to participate in the walk-a-thon. One friend did buy a property with Rebecca, but she feels the friend would have used her services anyway.

Summary. Rebecca feels adrift in the marketing of her listings and in herself as a REALTOR®. She wants to plan a cohesive marketing strategy that helps her brand herself in her agent marketplace. She believes that this can best be accomplished by concentrating her efforts on developing an image of someone who honestly cares about her community. She also wants to incorporate this self-promotion into her goals of providing outstanding service to her clients through the use of better marketing tools and useful consumer education. She has heard many stories of buyer and seller leads coming from the Internet and has decided to invest more of her 200Y marketing budget in this medium.

REBECCA'S PLAN FOR YEAR 200Y

After reviewing and evaluating the results of her 200X marketing activities, Rebecca is now working on her marketing program for the year 200Y. She has completed her research and is now ready to develop her marketing plan. After giving it much careful thought, Rebecca has developed this mission statement.

As a full-time, full-service real estate agent, I am committed to developing and implementing a niche market that includes educating the real estate consumer with breast cancer or recovering breast cancer survivor to better understand the transaction process as well as giving back to the communities where the consumer lives and works.

Rebecca's "niche" is her commitment to women's breast cancer awareness. More specifically, to women breast cancer survivors in Chicagoville.

Her goals are to

- create name recognition for herself within the community while providing service to the public and generating interest in her favorite charities;
- expand and improve her use of marketing tools; and
- revise her marketing materials and activities to be more interesting and creative.

As seen in the following, she has defined the actions she will take to reach each of these goals. Her next step will be to work out the details required to carry out each of the actions. When the plan is complete, she will find it easy to follow the steps she has outlined. After working her plan, she will then take time to measure the results and evaluate the 200Y plan in preparation for year 200Z.

Rebecca's Marketing Plan

Step 1: Determine the Purpose or Mission

Rebecca's new mission statement will become her purpose. She feels that providing excellent consumer education to her clients while contributing time and service to her favorite charities will not only enhance her image within the community but will expand her client base. Rebecca has developed a new motto: *"Rebecca Salesleader, contributing full time to Chicagoville, the community you'll want to call home."*

Other mottos that she considered were as follows:

- "Rebecca makes Chicagoville work for you."
- "Rebecca Salesleader proudly serving Chicagoville—full service and full time."
- "Let Rebecca Salesleader prove why Chicagoville should be your next town."

Step 2: Establish the Goals to Be Set in Order to Achieve the Purpose.

Rebecca has determined her four Ps of Marketing as follows:

- ***Product:*** Rebecca has two products: (1) Rebecca Salesleader, herself and (2) Rebecca Salesleader's listings.

- *Price:* Full commission with 10 percent of Rebecca's commission donated to Breast Cancer Foundation, Habitat for Humanity, or Chicagoville Regional Theater Company.
- *Placement:* Rebecca will respond within two business hours to all messages received by voice mail, live telephone calls, e-mails, or faxes.
- *Public Relations/Promotions:* Rebecca will use press releases and free workshops for consumer education plus sponsorship of issues and events that relate to her personal interests.

The Marketing Plan Goals

Goal #1. Gain name recognition within the community while providing consumer information to the public and supporting her favorite charities: Breast Cancer Foundation and Chicagoville Regional Theater Company.

Actions:

- *New Service Publicity:* Draft press release describing virtual tours of listed properties, and how these tours help buyers geographically separated from the market become acquainted with prospective homes. Educate the consumer about the process and technology of virtual tours and about how to go to Rebecca Salesleader's Web site to take a tour.

   Cost: Minimal (only time for preparing the release)

- *Consumer Education:*
   1. Hold four "What You Should Know About Mold" seminars in conference space at brokerage office. The local health department may have someone available for mak-

ing presentations on environmental issues like lead-based paint or mold. If not, look for a close-by company certified to remove mold to make a presentation. There is also a great deal of information available through both the National Association of REALTORS® and local REALTOR® associations. Issue press release to media with who, what, when, why, and where.

Cost: Marketing—none (unless decide to advertise in newspaper), $25 for coffee and snacks × 4 sessions = $100

2. Hold six "New Homebuyer Seminars" with mortgage broker who helped fund "Rebecca's Market Update" newsletter. Have virtual tours running on computers, have volunteer sign-up sheets for Habitat for Humanity, and informational handouts on hazards of mold and breast cancer awareness seminars. Have copies of newsletter and Rebecca Salesleader brochure available.

Cost: Coffee and snacks—6 sessions × 100 = $600

■ *Issue Sponsorship:* Hold two breast cancer awareness workshops in conference space at brokerage that educate the public on treatments, survivorship, and community resources available for breast cancer patients. Issue press release to media with who, what, when, why, and where. Feature that 10 percent of every commission earned by Rebecca will be donated to Breast Cancer Foundation.

Cost: Marketing: none (unless newspaper advertising), $25 for coffee and snacks × 2 sessions: = $50

■ *Event Sponsorship:* Buy a table at Chicagoville Regional Theater Company annual gala; invite aspiring high school theater actors to be guests. Issue press release to media looking for high school students to submit 500-word essay on why they would want to come as Rebecca's guests to gala.

Cost: Table = $800

- **Public Relations:** Rebecca will use the press release and media interest to solicit invitations for radio and newspaper interviews about the results of the 500-word essay contest for aspiring high school actors to receive theater gala tickets sponsored by Rebecca Salesleader.

  Cost: None

- **Media Kit:** Rebecca will distribute a media kit at all events. Kit will contain her resume, information about her company, Rebecca Salesleader information, and press releases in a professionally printed two-pocket folder.

  Cost: $100

Goal #2: Improve skills in marketing techniques; i.e., telemarketing, direct mail, Internet, and print advertising.

Actions:

- **Telemarketing:** Recognizing that the Do-Not-Call Registry strongly limits making outgoing cold calls, learn to make better use of office floor time. Sign up for local REALTOR® association seminar on "Making the Most of Floor Time."

  Cost: $35

  If no course is available, work on self-improvement by following these six sips for successful floor time:

1. Make it a point to *tour all of the office's listings* prior to designated floor time in order to speak positively and knowledgeably about any one of the properties listed.

2. *Arrive early* in time to get organized: have information on properties listed today in newspaper and in local homes magazine, listing sheets for similar properties to those advertised, and appointment book ready for scheduling follow-ups. Remember that buyers usually "buy up" from ads (Yes, that four-bedroom home at that low price really was too good to be true!) and "buy down" from signs (Yes, that is a truly beautiful home that you drove by, but it costs three times what you had hoped!).

3. *Smile!* Try placing a small mirror in front of the telephone as a reminder to smile. (It really does make a difference in how you come across to the caller.) Be enthusiastic and show that you appreciate the call. This is your only chance at a "first impression."

4. *Take careful notes* on the caller's name, phone number, and questions. If the questions can't be answered immediately, offer to get the information and call back. Even if it is days, or even weeks, later, be sure to make the return call.

5. *Show respect.* Don't irritate the caller by always answering a question with another question. "Does this house have a garage? Did you want a garage?" Answer the question and then follow up with an open-ended question. "Does this house have a garage? No, actually this particular property does not have a garage. Do you think a carport would suit your needs? If not, we have several other properties listed that do have a garage."

6. *Remember–the goal is to obtain an appointment.* Endeavor to talk about how the caller can be represented in the transaction, to show a specific property, to demonstrate vir-

tual tours, whatever. The main point is to convince the caller of the benefit of making an appointment to meet in person in order to best serve the caller's needs.

■ *Direct mail:* Create a bimonthly newsletter named, "Rebecca's Market Update" that includes the following eight topics:

1. All transactions closed in last month including time on the market and list versus sale price
2. Just listed properties and properties currently for sale
3. Story about Rebecca's Web site
4. Ad for mortgage lender—a paid insertion
5. Return coupon for free Comparative Market Analysis or finance information
6. General newsletter feedback
7. Theater ticket give-away to build response from newsletter
8. Promote mold and breast cancer awareness seminars, virtual tours, high school students essay contest, theater gala

Cost: $800

The newsletter content will contain the first seven items above as standard for each month and the 14 topics below will be featured in different months:

1. Masthead with Rebecca Salesleader market update, with contact information, month, and year
2. Short text paragraph about market conditions from her perspective
3. Table with sold properties, including address, list price, sold price, number of rooms, bedrooms, and baths
4. Request for relocation outbound referrals
5. Current listings of Rebecca's with property photos and descriptions

6. Mortgage rate update
7. Testimonials from current or closed clients
8. Market expectations in Chicagoville for the next year, with quotes from local board of REALTORS®
9. Community profile of neighboring town
10. Article about 500-word essay contest for high school students to attend regional theater company gala as Rebecca's guest, theme of contest, how to submit entries, etc.
11. Photo of Rebecca's Web site home page with description of content
12. Invitation to breast cancer awareness workshop with date, time, guest speaker biography, location, how to sign up, etc.
13. Article on current Habitat for Humanity project, interview with project director and new homeowners
14. Article on proposed new shopping centers, schools, hospitals, etc., in area

- *Internet:*
   1. *Web site:* Expand Web site from one page to five pages with first page for general information (picture, office address, and telephone, cell-phone, and fax numbers, link to e-mail address, one or two featured listings); a second page for current "Rebecca's Properties for Sale," and other attractive listings in the area; a page featuring the virtual tour gallery; a page for "Rebecca's Market Update" including link for "Sign up here for Rebecca's Market Update" sent by e-mail, fax, or snail mail; and a general community information page to post names of essay contest winners along with their essays, information on up-coming seminars on mold and for first-time home-

buyers, and other articles to promote breast cancer awareness.

Cost: $500

2. *E-Mail Marketing:* Purchase e-mail list of persons requesting information and computer program to send 1,000 e-mail advertising messages a month.

Cost: $600

(Stay up to date on antispam legislation. E-mail marketing is being limited to those persons with whom you already have a relationship. For example, the names on a sphere-of-influence list, or list of past clients and customers.)

3. *New domain name:* Purchase new (*rebeccashomes.com*) domain name for Rebecca's Web site by doing the following:
   – Select, check availability of, and purchase domain name at *networksolutions.com* (takes about 20 minutes to select and purchase a domain name).
   – Rely on *networksolutions.com* to give you alternatives if the name you select is already taken.
   – Don't use the word REALTOR® in your domain name.
   – Choose a name that is descriptive of what you do and who you are.
   – Recall that shorter is better and more memorable.
   – Keep "dots" and multiple words in your domain name to a minimum.

Cost: $50

4. *Virtual tours of listings:* Offer sellers virtual tours of their properties at no cost to them as unique selling point ver-

sus competition for the listing. When designing your virtual tours, remember the following:

- Good virtual tours work best in rooms or spaces wider than ten feet. Interior rooms with no windows or architectural features do not show well in virtual tours.
- Because windows and views outside of them photograph as blurred or hazy, don't plan on the best beach shot from inside a building. The camera should be set up outside to capture a view best.
- Pick the best four rooms: A good virtual tour should capture the flavor of a home and motivate the buyer to see it in person.
- Street shots that are 360 degrees help the buyer visualize the neighborhood.
- Many homes are purchased through virtual tours. Often the husband or wife is out of the country, and in a fast market decisions must be made quickly.
- Usually, computers built before 1995 can't handle the download of virtual tours. Virtual tours take longer with dial-up than with DSL.
- Virtual tour models are basically the same, except the number of shoots in standard packages vary by vendor. Too many shots can kill a potential showing. Less is more. Whet the appetite for a showing.

Cost: 75×12 listings = $900

- **■ *Print advertising:***
  1. *Reformat listing ads:* Rebecca knows her ads need more "pizzazz." She will include the following tips:
     - Focus on what you are selling—your listings and yourself.

- Increase white space—don't make ads too busy.
- Decrease font styles to two.
- Make bold headline and footer.
- Include client testimonials.

Rebecca will look for a graphic designer with professional experience, software and computer knowledge, who is a recipient of design awards and has good references.

2. *Place ad in women's business directory:* Research regional women-to-women business directory and purchase listing with the following wording:

Rebecca Salesleader, ABC Real Estate, Chicagoville, IL (847) 555-2000. rebecca@rebeccachicago.com. Proudly serving women in the purchase or sale of a home. Call or e-mail today to receive at no cost Rebecca's "Market Update" newsletter.

Cost: $75

3. *Redesign fax cover sheet:* Place tagline across top for online sign-up for "Rebecca's Market Update" newsletter. Tag across bottom of fax cover for free seminars, with topics and dates and with new Web site address (see Figure 6.1).

Cost: $25

4. *Ad in Chicagoville Regional Theater playbill:* Place ad promoting 500-word essay contest for interested high school theater students, as well as Rebecca's Web site address (see Figure 6.2).

Cost: $300

FIGURE 6.1 / Rebecca Salesleader's New Fax Cover Sheet

Call to receive Rebecca's "Market Update" newsletter at no cost!

FACSIMILE TRANSMITTAL

TO: FAX NUMBER:

FROM: **Rebecca Salesleader,**
                         ABC Real Estate
                         123 Main Street, Chicagoville, IL 60015
                         847-555-2000 Fax: 847-555-8009
                         E-mail: *Rebecca@rebeccachicago.com*
                         http://www.rebeccachicago.com

Insert body of Fax here:

_____

_____

_____

_____

_____

_____

_____

• *Sign up today for Rebecca's free breast cancer workshop on*
  April 28th, guest speaker Dianne Forman, Executive Director,
  Chicagoville Health Department

ABC
REAL ESTATE

FIGURE 6.2 / Rebecca Salesleader's Playbill Ad

Let Rebecca Salesleader take the drama out of your next home purchase or sale!

Call or e-mail for her
"Market Update" newsletter.
847-555-2000
Rebecca@rebeccachicago.com

 Rebecca Salesleader,
ABC Real Estate,
Chicagoville, IL 60015

Attention theater students! Submit an essay in 500 words or less on why you should be one of five lucky guests at her table for the Chicagoville Regional Theater Company's Black Tie Gala. *Hurry!* The essay deadline is April 30, 200X.

Goal #3: Revise personal marketing materials and activities to catch the attention of the public.

Actions:

- *Business card and agent brochure:* Develop new card (see Figure 6.3) look emphasizing new domain name and agent brochure (see Figure 6.4) to leave for takeaway at public open houses.

  Cost: $200

FIGURE 6.3 / Sample Business Card

rebecca@rebeccachicago.com
http://www.rebeccachicago.com
http://www.realestate.com

Rebecca Salesleader
Broker Associate

ABC REAL ESTATE
123 Main Street, Chicagoville, IL 60015
Office: (847) 555-2000 • Cell: (847) 555-3333
Pager: (847) 555-4448 • Fax: (847) 555-8009

Because less is more, keep design elements simple, including just the following information, plus company logo:

- Name, title—broker, sales associate, salesperson, company logo
- Office name, street address
- Office phone, cell phone, pager, home office numbers
- Fax number
- Agent Web site address
- Company Web site address
- E-mail address
- Photo (optional)

■ ***Business to business:*** Reformat "Rebecca's Market Update" newsletter to send to real estate attorneys, title companies, home inspectors, appraisers, mortgage brokers every quarter to build business to business referrals.

Cost: $250

FIGURE 6.4 / Sample Brochure

Rebecca Salesleader,
Broker Associate

A broker associate with ABC Real Estate with
five year's experience in the Chicagoville market,
Rebecca enjoys working with first-time homebuyers,
relocation clients, or neighbors looking to find a
larger home for their growing family. Rebecca makes
the Chicagoville market work for them.

Rebecca's strong market presence comes from a full-time commitment to her real
estate business and clients. Her skills in helping people purchase or sell single-family
homes, townhouses, condominiums, new construction, and vacant land in all price
ranges make her an award-winning sales agent with ABC Real Estate.

Recognizing the importance of the Internet with real estate consumers, she hosts
rebeccachicago.com, where her current property listings, community information,
weather, and commuting times are available 24/7. Rebecca also hosts a page on her
brokerage Web site *ABCRealEstate.com* where all properties listed with her company
as well as links to the local multiple-listing service and *realtor.com* are available. Take a
virtual tour of one of her listings at your leisure on her Web site. Rebecca's virtual
tours feature a curbside photo plus four additional 360-degree videos of interior
rooms of her listings.

Giving back to the Chicagoville community is important to Rebecca. She understands
how much her clients have given to her throughout her career in real estate in
Chicagoville. As a volunteer for the Chicagoville chapter of Habitat for Humanity, she
appreciates the hard work they contribute to new low-income homeowners so they
can realize their dream of home ownership.

The Chicagoville Regional Theater Company also gives Rebecca a chance to explore
her interest in theater. With her education in interior design, she brings a creative edge
to the set design of this growing reputable theater company. As a board member of the
theater company, her business experience and contacts within Chicagoville help make
it one of the most profitable companies in the Chicagoville area.

Rebecca is your one-stop real estate professional in Chicagoville. Call her today to find
property information, to get a free market analysis, or to talk about your housing
needs, today, tomorrow, or next year.

ABC Real Estate, Chicagoville, IL 60015

■ ***Public open houses:*** Have virtual tour of property running on computer during open house to illustrate its use. Offer door prizes as incentive in open house ad to build traffic. Have copies of "Rebecca's Market Update" and Rebecca Salesleader brochures available. Have volunteer sign up sheets for Habitat for Humanity, handouts for new homebuyer, mold, and breast cancer awareness seminars at open houses.

Cost: 12 open houses × $25 = $300

■ ***Hold housewarmings with closed clients:*** Using this innovative way to generate new leads, Rebecca can say thanks to present clients and meet new ones all in one day. Rebecca holds a housewarming for six of her buyers. Rebecca sends invitations to between 25 and 40 of the new owner's friends and family, works with the clients to decide on menu, and orders food through local caterer. Rebecca picks up the food and helps set up. When the party starts, so does the networking.

Cost: $200 each × 6 = $1,200

■ ***Brag book:*** Include the following items in a book that can be left with prospective clients:
   – Thank-you letters from clients
   – Sales awards or recognitions
   – Samples of listing advertising: listing sheets, brochures, newspaper ads, broker to broker advertising; i.e., "Come to Broker's Open House for my new listing at: XXX Green Street, Chicagoville, lunch served." Include print version of personal and brokerage Web site with agent and listings featured.
   – CD-ROM copy of virtual tour from previous listing

Cost: $50

Rebecca has chosen two additional activities to broaden her own networking sphere and receive further education. She will join the Women's Council of REALTORS® in order to network with other REALTORS® in the region to build referrals for potential clients coming into Rebecca's market.

Cost: $50

She has also decided to attain the Graduate REALTOR® Institute (GRI) Designation. In addition to receiving the additional education for herself, she believes that real estate consumers and other GRIs will now refer business to her based on the perception of value for ongoing education.

Cost: $375

The total costs for Rebecca Salesleader's year 200Y marketing plan is $9,960 or 10 percent of gross revenue from previous year 200X.

IN CONCLUSION

Rebecca has mapped out an ambitious program that she plans to follow in the coming year in order to reach her goals to

- create name recognition for herself within the community while providing service to the public and generating interest in her favorite charities;
- expand and improve her use of marketing tools; and
- revise her marketing materials and activities to be more interesting and creative.

She has developed her action plan for each of the goals. She will now need to write out the specific details necessary in order to implement each of the actions; i.e., whom to contact, where to send materials, etc. She will also need to set up a timeline with deadlines for completion of each activity. Obviously, she cannot complete everything in her plan in the first month of the year. She will need to prioritize and to see how the development of one action—for example, the new format for her business cards—can be used as part of other actions, such as preparing the layout for her personal brochure, newsletter, Web site, and other print advertising.

She will now be ready for Step Three—Implementing the Plan; that is, "Just do it!" At the end of the year she'll be ready for Step Four——Evaluating the Results by making another detailed market audit. That audit will clearly show her which new ideas worked well and which had not been worth the time and money. Based on this input from year 200Y she will be ready to start working on her marketing plan for 200Z!

Putting It All in Practice
Field Exercises

CHAPTER 1
Making the Most of Your First Line of Marketing—You!

1. Make a list of the top three things you feel you have to offer a customer or client. Do you have special education or credentials to back this up?

2. Select five people who know you well and have them write down the answers to the following question:

   What are the top three things about _____ *(you) that make him or her an outstanding real estate agent?*

   Following are suggested people to ask:

   ■ Your managing broker
   ■ Your favorite past client

- Your significant other
- A close friend
- An office acquaintance

Compare and contrast your top-three-things list to theirs. Are they the same? Did some of their answers surprise you? Did some of their answers disappoint you? If their lists are not the same as yours, would you rather work toward the points they raised or work harder to make your original list more dynamic?

What steps will you take to reinforce the three things that you would like to be considered a part of your image?

3. Prepare your sphere-of-influence list (a minimum of 200 names), including names, addresses, contact numbers, and e-mail addresses. Develop a system for contacting each of the names on your list at a minimum of every three months. Pick out specific holidays, birthday, or anniversary dates to incorporate into your system. Decide whether to use a special computer software program, Excel spreadsheet, or other way to track the type of contact, when it was made, and any resulting response. It does not really matter whether you choose to have a file box of 3 × 5 cards, or a more elaborate Excel program. Just decide on a system that you know will be easy for you to use and maintain.

4. Make a list of community activities in which you have been involved in the past year. What will you do for them this year? Are there new or different activities you would like to be a part of? How much financial commitment are you willing to make? How much time are you willing to give?

CHAPTER 2
Delivering Your Message

1. Pick a week and for several consecutive days, pay attention to the general advertisements (department stores, book stores, health clubs, etc.) you see in the newspaper or other print resource. Write down which ones catch your attention, which ones you like, which ones you do not like, and why. Study each one and decide if it is intended to promote the product alone, or is the ad saying that "we know you and this is why this product is best for you"? Which of these ads would make you consider buying their product? Why?

2. Review the list of potential niche markets listed below. Which of these could be a possible niche market for you? Why? Review your current list of clients. Are you already working in a niche market? If so, outline the activities you will use this year to make better contact with this group. If you do not presently have a niche market, select one of the following and outline an action plan to develop your new market:

   - Senior citizens
   - Immigrants
   - Nationality
   - Gender
   - Single parent head of households
   - Community interest organizations
   - Protected classes
   - Political groups
   - Professional
   - Spiritual
   - Sexual preference

- Military
- International clients

3. Review your activities over the past year by asking the following questions:

- Is there anything that would have been good for a press release?
- Did you take part in a special community activity?
- Were you involved in Habitat for Humanity or other nonprofit group projects?
- Did you sponsor a sports team at one of the local schools?
- Did you speak at a chamber of commerce, Rotary, or other organization meeting?

Try writing a press release based on one of these activities. Prepare a cover letter to send with the press release and decide which newspaper would have been an appropriate choice to receive it.

In the coming year, think about the possibilities for a press release as you take part in special activities. Always take pictures at the event–preferably of you with one of the recipients of any benefits being offered. Send the picture along with your cover letter and press release. Be sure to keep track of any responses you receive based on the article.

CHAPTER 3
Developing a Marketing Plan

1. Set a financial goal for yourself for the next year (the year can start in any month, not necessarily a calendar year). Use the following to make the goal specific:

- I will earn _____ from my real estate practice in the coming year.
- My average commission will be _____.
- It will take _____ successful transactions to reach my financial goal. (Divide total to be earned by your average commission.)
- To have a total of 30 transactions for the year, I will need an average of _____ closings per month.

For Example To earn $100,000 with an average commission of $3,000, it will take 30 transactions—either a sold listing or a sale. This will require an average of 2.5 closings per month.

2. Is your goal realistic? Only you can answer this. But if your income was $24,000 last year, your new goal of $100,000 may not be realistic. Remember to take into account any periods of time that you will be out of the market (long vacation, maternity leave, caring for child or parent, etc.).

3. Is your goal measurable? Any goal depending on numbers is totally measurable. If the goal is 2.5 closings per month, they could be tracked in the following way:

MONTH	GOAL	ACTUAL
January	2.5	2.5
February	2.5	2.0
March	3.0	3.0
April	2.5	4.0
May	2.5	

When the goal is not reached, add the difference to the next month. If the goal is exceeded, this is "gravy." The goal for the next month remains the same.

4. Prepare a marketing budget for the next year. Remember to include all forms of media advertising, direct mailings, cost of cards, brochures, signs, etc. The standard rule of thumb is 10 percent of income:

$100,000 income goal × .10 = $10,000 marketing budget.

CHAPTER 4
Marketing Tools and Techniques

1. Select one of your listings. Write an ad that uses visual, auditory, and kinesthetic words, all in the same ad.

2. Make a list of the marketing tools you used last year. Which one produced the most prospects? Which one did you enjoy doing the most? Which ones will you continue to use this year? What new ones will you experiment with?

3. Write ads for three catalogs that feature marketing tools like postcards, calendars, prepared brochures or newsletters, and give-away incentives. Pick out the ones that you will use to contact your sphere-of-influence list.

4. See if there is a real estate channel on cable TV in your area. Call for information on how listings are prepared for submission, type of contract required, and cost.

CHAPTER 5
21st-Century Marketing

1. Make a list of the technology tools you use at present: cell phone, fax, laptop, desktop, PDA. Are they up-to-date models? Establish an order of priority for replacing outdated ones.

2. Plan your own Web site. Read the list of Web content ideas listed in Chapter 5. Pick the ones that you will include in your Web site and decide in which of the top search engines you will have your Web site "seeded."

3. Contact a virtual tour company and Web site designer for an estimate of cost and information on what to set up on your new Web site, including the virtual tour aspect.

4. Prepare an e-mail address list. Group names by categories so that you can send out the same message to many people at once.

5. Set up an automatic responder for when you are out of touch for as much as a day. Be sure you have a signature including all of your contact information that automatically prints at the bottom of outgoing messages. For help with this, click on the "help" button on your e-mail provider.

6. Use the Internet to obtain information that can be used in your newsletter. Check out *http://www.realtor.org* and your own state and local REALTOR® association Web sites. For useful demographic data look at *http://www.census.gov*. This site can also be helpful when determining a niche market. For com-

munity activities, pull up your local chamber of commerce Web site and any parks and recreation sites for your area.

Implementing the Marketing Plan

1. Using Rebecca's plan as a guide, prepare your own detailed marketing plan for the year. Write down each step including deadlines for each action. Remember to include the following:

- Decide on a stated purpose or mission.
- Determine at least four goals that will help you fulfill your mission. Add a deadline for each action to be completed.
- Under each goal, write out at least four actions to be taken. Include a completion deadline for each action.
- Details, details, details are at the heart of making actions happen. Take each of the actions you have listed under each of your goals and think through all of the details that will be necessary in order for that action to be accomplished. Put in a deadline for each detail to be completed.

Each goal of your marketing plan layout should look like Figure 7.1:

FIGURE 7.1 / Marketing Plan Worksheet

Goal #1: _____

	Deadline
Action #1: _____	_____

Details

1) _____   _____

2) _____   _____

3) _____   _____

4) _____   _____

Action #2: _____   _____

Details

1) _____   _____

2) _____   _____

3) _____   _____

4) _____   _____

Action #3: _____   _____

Details

1) _____   _____

2) _____   _____

3) _____   _____

4) _____   _____

Repeat for each action in Goal #1, then make chart for Goal #2, #3, and #4.

Appendix
Web Sites

A

Agent stationary/business cards, color postcards
http://www.printingedgemarketing.com

Agent Web sites
http://www.agentimage.com

Airport billboards
http://www.outofamerica.com

B

Billboard advertising
http://www.billboardsetc.com

Bus shelter billboards
http://www.gatewayoutdoor.com

Bus stop bench advertising
http://www.bench-ad.com

Brochure boxes
http://www.reboxes.com

C

CD-ROM property marketing
http://www.brochureondemand.com

Car signs
http://www.homesalez.com

Clip art
http://www.realestateclipart.com

Create postcards, flyers
http://www.hp.com/sbso/solutions/real/marketing_assistant.html

D

Digital cameras
http://www.hp.com/sbso/solutions/real/pg_digital_cameras.html

Direct response programs
http://www.hobbsherder.com

Domain registration
http://www.networksolutions.com
http://www.realtown.com/resources/index.aspx

E

E-mail hosting
http://www.realtown.com/resources/index.aspx

Everything real estate
http://www.everythingre.com

I

Internet corporation for assigned names
http://www.icann.org

Internet marketing general
http://www.eneighborhoods.com

Indoor billboards parking garages
http://www.adwalls.com

Internet newsletters
http://www.realtown.com/resources/index.aspx

Internet search engine optimization
http://www.paloalto.com

L

Lead generation
http://www.rechannel.com

Listing yard sign hotline phone numbers
http://www.877infoline.com/sale2.html

Listservs
http://www.realtown.com/resources/index.aspx

M

Magnet for marketing
http://www.magnetstreet.com

Marketing plan software
http://www.paloalto.com

Mobile billboards
http://www.outofamerica.com

N

Network solutions—domain name purchase, hosting, Web sites
http://www.networksolutions.com

O

Online showing feedback
http://www.homefeedback.com

P

Postcards
http://www.postcardpress.com

Purchase online community bulletin board
http://www.realtown.com/resources/index.aspx

R

Real estate blog
http://www.morningstarmultimedia.com/realestate/index.as

Real estate letters
http://www.myrealestateletters.com

Real estate link exchange
http://www.realestatelinkexchange.com

Real estate advertising items superstore
http://www.4realestateagent.com

REALTOR® use in a domain name
http://www.useofrealtorinadomain.realtown.com

T

Telephone applications for real estate agents
http://www.easyivr.com/aprealestate.htm

Trade show materials
http://www.renaissance-media.com

V

Virtual tours
http://www.visualtour.com/uses.asp

W

Web hosting
http://www.realtown.com/resources/index.aspx
http://www.networksolutions.com

Web marketing
http://www.virtual-agent.com

Y

Yard signs
http://www.realestatesigns.com

Index